Wealth Creation and Justice

The World Council of Churches' Encounters

with the

World Bank

and the

International Monetary Fund

Report of the First Encounter
Geneva, 13-14 February 2003

edited by
Rogate R. Mshana

WCC Publications, Geneva

This document is the report of the WCC/WB/IMF first encounter which took place in Geneva, Switzerland, 13-14 February 2003. It will also serve as a background paper to the WCC/World Bank/IMF second encounter, 28-29 October 2003, in Washington D.C., USA.

Contents

Foreword

*Konrad Raiser**

Discussions between representatives of the World Council of Churches and the two most important international financial institutions are by no means self-evident. The WCC is known for having articulated critical views of the international financial system and the policies pursued by the World Bank and IMF. Many among the constituency of the WCC, particularly in the southern hemisphere, would question the wisdom and purpose of dialogue. For their part, the World Bank and the IMF expressed interest in meeting and eventually cooperating with leaders of religious communities in order to enlist their support in addressing the challenges arising from economic and financial globalization. They have been hesitant, however, to enter into discussions about the fundamental assumptions underlying their policies.

The first seminar involving the three organizations therefore brought together people who have so far had little opportunity to talk face to face. At a time when economic and financial globalization has become a very contentious issue, participants helped create a space in which difficult issues concerning the sustainability of the global human community can be faced with respect for the integrity of one another's convictions and commitments.

The WCC has no pretensions of superior insight and technical knowledge about the complex realities of economic and financial globalization. While ecumenical discussion on the issues of a just economic order has been informed all along by the insight and advice of competent experts, it has primarily sought to articulate the voice of those who have little opportunity of influencing the decisions, but have to bear their consequences. Some of these experiences entered the dialogue and gave it the human face which is a central focus of the discussion.

Given the complexity of the issues under discussion and the significant difference in the outlook of participants, the first seminar can only be a beginning. It is my sincere hope that it will have convinced us that a continuation is of mutual interest. While we cannot expect quick results, it is a significant step to establish a basis for continuing conversation and eventually to prepare for an encounter between the leadership of the respective organizations.

---

* Konrad Raiser is general secretary of the WCC.

Introduction

*Rogate R. Mshana**

The first seminar between the World Council of Churches (WCC), the World Bank and the International Monetary Fund (IMF) took place in Geneva in February 2003, with thirty participants and observers. This seminar was the first of three planned to take place within two years. The third meeting, scheduled for 2004, will be between the governing bodies of all three institutions.

To begin with, the WCC had been invited by senior officials of the IMF to enter into discussions about development issues. In response, the general secretary of the WCC, in letters to the president of the World Bank and the managing director of the IMF, suggested the need for encounters between the institutions that would discuss fundamental questions about world development today.

A meeting of staff from all three organizations was held in May 2002 to plan for these encounters. The meeting commenced with a rich exchange of information on institutional histories and mandates, as well as a presentation on the background and objectives of the encounters. The WCC highlighted its continuing work on economic justice and its vision of sustainable human development. The World Bank shared its dream of 'a world free from poverty' and ongoing work on the World Faiths Development Dialogue (WFDD). The IMF emphasized the importance of involving more people in the poverty reduction strategy process (PRSP). It emerged that the WCC, World Bank and IMF share the common objective of eradicating poverty, based on the values and ethics of life. However, it was acknowledged that their philosophies of development are not the same. It was also recognized that the three institutions have shown adaptability and sensitivity in responding to global issues, not least in their willingness to exchange ideas and experiences. It was agreed that the encounters between the institutions should be innovative, involve a definite process, and lead to something new.

The seminar of February 2003 had two main objectives: (1) to enable all three institutions to look critically at their mandates and their approach to development; (2) to raise fundamental questions for further debate. Wealth creation, social justice and the commodification of public goods, such as water, were also discussed.

Part of the rationale for the encounters is to explore differences in overall worldview and how these are translated into action, given the limits imposed by respective structures of governance and mandates. The participation of leaders of the three organizations will be an important and symbolic gesture at the culmination of the whole process. Issues for discussion in the seminars include:

- institutional governance;
- ethics and equity, and how they can guide markets and finance;
- the responsibility and accountability of institutional actors;
- economics as a matter of faith (*Oikos*);
- sustainability.

*Rogate R. Mshana is Programme Executive for Economic Justice with the WCC.

1

Beginnings

Bob Goudzwaard

In January 2002 the first formal step was taken to begin a series of encounters between the WCC, World Bank and IMF. Konrad Raiser – then general secretary of the World Council of Churches – wrote a letter to James Wolfensohn of the World Bank and Horst Köhler of the IMF in which he said:

> Believing that there are alternatives to the current global economic system, and concerned about the basic ethical values which are at stake, the WCC wants to respond positively to the suggestion of your institutions to enter into a serious dialogue... about the fundamental questions regarding world development today.

The three institutions share a long history of mutual wariness: twenty years ago, perhaps even ten years ago, a meeting would have been impossible. Add to that our differences in background, life experiences and worldviews, then a question poses itself quite naturally: why now? What has changed to make encounters like the ones we have begun seem useful to all three of us?

Two answers come to mind. The first is a common awareness of *urgency*. Severe problems confront the world today. Of course, poverty, sustained indebtedness and the destruction of the environment are nothing new, but they are more structurally embedded than ever before, and are increasingly accepted by a majority as almost self-evident phenomena, even facts of life. This fatalism is basically untenable for all three institutions and we cannot give in to it. It also brings us closer together than we have ever been. Selfish neglect of the welfare of common people and reluctance to act responsibly are our common enemies.

The second answer involves a shared sense of *relevancy*. We live amid rapid, perhaps unstable, globalization. New ideas and concepts of development have come to the fore. Can we, should we, influence the direction of present developments? In his reply to Konrad Raiser's letter, James Wolfensohn wrote that all of us are development actors. We all share the role and destiny of being such actors today. The series of encounters we have begun is the first time in modern history that the oldest actor on the global stage will meet directly with the most representative – and far more powerful – new global actors. The Christian church, almost two millennia ago, began a form of worldwide engagement, deeply related to the well-being of the whole inhabited world. It is this world that is now at stake.

Will we succeed in our efforts? Will we have any lasting influence on each other? The answer to both these questions is yes, providing we remember our common goal: a sustainable future for the whole of creation. Our individual orientations, our judgements about the world, must not be elevated beyond all doubt and discussion. We must be open to the possibility of change, if we are really to meet present and future challenges.

A meaningful, lasting encounter between the WCC, World Bank and the IMF requires at least three conditions.

First, we must be willing to listen carefully to each other if we wish to be innovative and to continue in the process already begun – the global issues of our time require adaptability and sensitivity.

Second, we must accept some degree of transparency. We should not meet simply for ourselves. Churches, for example, are nothing without their members, and our encounters are related to specific personal lives which may well be at stake. Feedback to our constituencies is essential.

Third, we should be willing to agree, but also, if necessary, to disagree. In other words, our purpose is not to convince each other of our own views. Non-agreement should not be regarded as failure. Instead, we must clarify our mutual positions, understand our various orientations, and have a clear eye for our own inherent weaknesses.

It is sometimes difficult to communicate with others, especially when their worldviews diverge from our own. However, despite such differences, there can be a common awareness of some kind of meaning beyond ourselves. Churches try to relate to an ultimate meaning, but they must remain aware that they lack any kind of ownership over it. The ecumenical pioneer John Oldham once said: 'Only as the Christian Gospel is brought into a close relationship with the realities and actual problems of the world today, [only then] can we expect mankind to recognize in it a living word of judgement and redemption.'

It is from this horizon of expectation that I wish all three institutions a fruitful series of encounters. I am sure that the outcome can be a successful one, if we combine hope and trust and greet each other respectfully.

2

Historical Overview of Ecumenical Debate about Development

Robert van Drimmelen

Although the word 'development' does not appear anywhere in the Bible, the concept of development was widely debated in ecumenical circles during the twentieth century, especially the 1970s and 1980s. In 1970 the WCC organized an important meeting in Montreux, Switzerland, where the issue of development was discussed and which led to the formation of the Commission on the Churches' Participation in Development (CCPD). The WCC was already involved in issues related to development, notably through CICARWS (the department for world service or 'international diaconia') and the activities of the programme on urban and rural mission. The CCPD was established to serve as a think-tank and laboratory to help put ecumenical reflection about development into action. Several WCC reorganizations later, the departments that originally dealt with development issues no longer exist. The basic concerns, however, are still on the agenda of the WCC. Development issues are now mainly addressed under the headings of globalization and justice, peace and creation.

The WCC does not have an 'official' social teaching (neither, for that matter, does it have an official theology). Rather, there is ecumenical debate about development. Thus, within the WCC and the ecumenical movement as a whole, different opinions exist about the issues at stake.

The missionary movement has mainly been responsible for putting the issue of development on the agenda of the churches. The best missionaries never created a dichotomy between the spiritual and the material aspects of life. The Gospel (the Good News) is meant for the human individual as a whole. Inviting people to turn to the living God includes efforts to improve their material conditions.

Initially, the ecumenical debate about development issues centred on certain unfortunate features and consequences of economic life. The basic structures which produced these consequences were not seriously questioned. The debate was more descriptive than analytical, more palliative than fundamental, and more remedial than a basic reshaping. Economic growth was seen as the engine of development and, indeed, sometimes equated with development and progress. Development was seen as a linear catching-up process: countries in the South should follow the example of the West. Therefore, there should be a transfer of knowledge, expertise, technology and resources from West to South. In this sense, the ecumenical debate was not much different from the secular debate on development.

In the course of time and as the participation of southern churches in the WCC increased, critical voices were raised. By the mid-1970s, the very idea of development was questioned by some in the ecumenical movement. Richard Dickinson identifies a number of characteristics of the ecumenical debate about development in the mid-1970s:[1]

1   The traditional understanding of development focused too narrowly on economic development per se and paid little attention to non-economic factors in social transformation, such as cultural and religious divisions.

2   Real social transformation was to be measured by what happens to people, while the traditional notions of development tended to emphasize more abstract economic or political objectives. In fact, the notion of people-centred development was soon to become the distinctive feature of the ecumenical understanding of development.

3   Many discussions on development appeared to assume a facile harmony of interests between the rich and the poor, while the real situation often was a conflict between the 'haves' and the 'have-nots'.

4   There was a growing conviction that, in the name of development, many national and international economic structures were perpetuating or even reinforcing structures of injustice. Thus, many prominent ecumenical ethicists gradually rejected 'development' altogether and chose instead to speak of 'liberation'.

5   Given the enormous strain on the environment, which growth models of development implied, many began to question whether the ideals of development were even suitable, attainable and desirable.

6   There was a growing awareness of the deficiencies of the traditional top-down approach in development theory: to rely heavily on 'trickle-down' seemed at best inefficient, at worst a hoax on the poor.

A key emphasis which emerged in ecumenical reflection and action concerning development in the mid-1970s was on the crucial role of participation. People should be the subjects of history, and justice should not merely be distributive but also participatory. 'The people', especially the marginalized and oppressed, should be able to participate in development. The quest for what was called a just, participatory and sustainable society (JPSS) embodied this conviction.

God's 'preferential option for the poor' and the emphasis on the poor as agents of development were worked out in a study process called 'Towards a Church in Solidarity with the Poor' (initially called 'Towards a Church of the Poor'). In practice, this led to greater attention to people's movements and networks between these movements, as well as more emphasis on contextual and 'micro' approaches, although 'macro' approaches were never totally forgotten. The commitment to solidarity with the poor led to some lively debates. Who are the poor? Should Christians endorse every action and strategy adopted by poor people? What is the relationship between poverty and righteousness?

From the mid-1980s onwards, justice, peace and the integrity of creation (JPIC) became the rallying theme of the WCC. The conciliar process of mutual commitment (covenant) to JPIC emphasized that Christian resistance against the powers of death is part and parcel of confessing Christ as the life of the world. Struggles for justice, peace and the integrity of creation cannot be separated – they need to be kept in a dynamic relationship. Because of this holistic approach, it has been argued that JPIC may be a better ecumenical term for development.[2]

During the 1990s, increasing emphasis was placed on environmental issues. Over and against the notion of sustainable development, which became popular in the context of the 1992 Earth Summit, the WCC emphasized sustainable communities, thereby elaborating the earlier concept of sustainable society. Sustainability, as the WCC understands it, does not mean global economic growth qualified by environmental sensitivity, but a primary emphasis on local and regional communities that are economically viable, socially quitable and ecologically renewable.[3]

The first half of the 1990s saw a multiplication of democratic associations at the level of civil society, strongly influencing the democratization of political structures, especially in the South. At the same time, the phenomenon of globalization intensified and became fully apparent. These three issues – globalization, the rise of (international) civil society, and sustainable communities – became an important focus in ecumenical debate.

What Have We Learned and Achieved?
It is difficult to identify and measure what the ecumenical movement has learned over the years about development. Measuring rods that can be used include pronouncements of governing bodies of the WCC, writings of prominent ecumenical ethicists, and, last but not least, the concrete actions of those involved in development-related activities. Some of the lessons learned may be obvious truths in hindsight: it is always easier to judge after the event than in an actual historical situation. Lessons learned and mistakes made cannot really be separated. What may have been learned has not always been applied in practice, nor was it always really 'owned' by mainline churches and development agencies.

Since its inception, the issue of human rights has been important for the WCC. Initially, its discussions largely focused on religious freedom as the entry point into human rights concerns. At the end of the 1960s, the debate broadened to include social and economic rights. Earlier attempts to defend the values of a 'Christian culture' as the only basis for freedom and justice in a responsible society gave way to a new appreciation of religious and cultural pluralism and a recognition of the need for a genuine dialogue between cultures.

Another important lesson learned is that economic growth as the paradigm for development is clearly insufficient. Over the decades, world production has grown, leading to enormous improvements and benefits for certain groups in society. However, as world production has grown, so has, in many cases, the gap between rich and poor. Moreover, in certain parts of the world and in certain economic sectors, economic growth has taken on the character of jobless growth, thereby contributing to more inequality and exclusion. For millions of destitute people, to *have* more is to *be* more. It is also clear that economic growth alone does not solve social problems. If economic growth is absolutely necessary to remove poverty, why has it not done so?

Of course, the ecumenical movement was not alone in discovering the fallacy of the trickle-down approach, which was dismissed by many theoreticians as well as practitioners. Nevertheless, this lesson has not 'trickled-up' to all decision-making powers and institutions.

The ecumenical movement has learned that there is a need to change our thinking and reverse our arguments. Why not consider whether policies aimed at poverty reduction, the generation of long-term employment, and environmental restoration and protection, will lead to economic growth? Such an approach contrasts with prevailing thought, which begins with economies and their growth and presupposes that the benefits will eventually trickle down to all layers of society. The reverse approach takes the needs of human beings and their communities ('the people') – present and future generations – and creation as a whole, as the starting point. In this line of thought, social policies are not seen as later correctives to the unfortunate outcomes of economic processes, or as an afterthought. Rather, social and environmental goals are the primary and integrated objectives, while economic growth might only be a by-product. What are now considered externalities' of economic processes would be internalized in the very economic processes themselves. People's participation, people's movements and civil society as a whole play a key role in this alternative approach.

The WCC has also gained a better understanding of the multifaceted meaning of development and the need for a comprehensive approach. People should be at the centre of development. Therefore, development should primarily be social development. It is in this field of social development that the ecumenical movement has made important contributions through its focus on community development projects and programmes, education and training, an emphasis on social justice, people's participation, the role of people's movements and their need for networking. More recently, this emphasis has been translated into efforts to probe the notion of civil society.

With its emphasis on people's participation, the ecumenical movement has been somewhat ahead of the secular debate, considering the fact that it was only in its Human Development Report of 1993 that the United Nations Development Programme (UNDP) put people's participation centre stage. The notion of participation introduced a clear political dimension into the debate, challenging hidden and overt technocratic and 'economistic' assumptions. It was realized, albeit only in the mid-1970s, that the traditional ecumenical debate about economic and social justice had to be broadened to include the dimension of political power.

There was also an early awareness of environmental concerns, which were raised at an ecumenical conference in Bucharest in 1974. It took a while, however, before such issues were actually taken up in specific programmes. Initially, there were tensions between those in the ecumenical movement who promoted a 'justice agenda' and those who advocated environmental concerns. The JPIC process contributed to a better understanding of these tensions and stimulated a more holistic approach.

The growing awareness of environmental concerns led to an even broader understanding of the issues at stake. In the context of its work on the UNCED follow-up process, the WCC advocated working towards the building of sustainable communities rather than sustainable development. The social idea of sustainable communities implies the nurturing of equitable relationships both within the human family and between humans and the ecological community as a whole. Such sustainable communities imply a just and moral economy where people are empowered to be involved in making decisions that affect their lives; where public and private institutions and enterprises are accountable and held responsible for the social and environmental impacts and consequences of their operations; and where the Earth and the whole created order are nurtured with utmost respect and reverence, rather than exploited and degraded.

By asserting the primacy of justice, ecological sustainability and the creation of viable communities, the ecumenical movement states that authentic human development can never be achieved when the ultimate goal is amassing wealth and material goods, especially when these are at the expense of others in the global community and of the health of the global environmental commons. Justice and equity must be at the heart of any sustainable economic, social or environmental system supporting the whole Earth community.[4]

Meanwhile, economic development was never totally rejected. It was, however, qualified by social and environmental imperatives. For example, in the early 1970s the WCC established Oikocredit (formerly called the Ecumenical Development Cooperative Society) to lend to commercially viable enterprises which comply with a set of social and environmental criteria. Much earlier, the Ecumenical Loan Fund (ECLOF) was established. Initially, it focused on the reconstruction of church buildings that were destroyed during the Second World War. Now, it provides low-interest loans to small business enterprises in the South. Churches and church-related organizations all over the world have set up or supported income-generating projects which contribute to economic development. In the field of micro-credits, the ecumenical movement arrived early on the scene.

The same may be true for the debate about the level of Official Development Assistance (ODA). While the United Nations adopted the target of 0.7 per cent of Gross National Product for ODA (the 1968 WCC Assembly in Uppsala had asked for 1 per cent), the WCC appealed to member churches to use a minimum of 2 per cent of their regular income from all sources for development purposes by 1971. Although this target was never achieved, the 2% Appeal generated an income of millions of dollars for the Ecumenical Development Fund (EDF). The EDF was instrumental in setting up Round Tables and consortia that provided fora for efforts to establish less unequal relationships between so-called donors and receivers. One-quarter of the EDF and the

2% Appeal was to be used for development education. Together with other WCC initiatives, such as the programme on ecumenical sharing of resources, this stimulated lively debate about the concept of 'partnership in development'. The ecumenical movement provided one of the very few international platforms for such a debate.

Despite this emphasis on the transfer of resources for social development projects, the ecumenical movement did not lose sight of the wider factors that profoundly influence success or failure at the micro level. Studies on macro issues were carried out by the WCC Advisory Group on Economic Matters, chaired by Jan Pronk. Issues addressed included the New International Economic Order, transnational corporations, food and hunger, employment and unemployment, and the international financial system. Late in the 1980s, the WCC embarked on a three-year participatory process which led to the study document on 'Christian Faith and the World Economy Today'. The insight that macro and micro aspects should be kept together in studies, education and actions, constitutes another important lesson. In addition, it was increasingly realized that development goes beyond charity and the transfer of money from the rich to the poor. Development requires justice, at home and abroad, and not only distributive justice, but also commutative justice based on participation. Emergency relief remains necessary but, wherever possible, it should be organized in a way which takes account of longer-term perspectives.

Although there is a strong prophetic tradition in the ecumenical movement aimed at unmasking and denouncing injustice, there is also the awareness that good prophets do not simply tell us what is wrong but also point us in the right direction. Resistance against injustice gains credibility when it is coupled with proposals for viable alternative arrangements. It was this philosophy that guided the policies of the EDF and was at the basis of Oikocredit. The long-term vision should not be lost, but it is only realistic not to expect immediate and dramatic changes. There is no 'development without tears' and those involved in promoting social development require much perseverance.

What Mistakes Have Been Made?
During the first decades of its existence, discussions in the WCC largely followed the international (development) agenda as formulated in the context of the United Nations. Thereby, it largely neglected a critical examination of the political realm and of the changing nature of power relations in society. Much work was done on economic, military and technological issues, but much less attention was given to the political conditions for effecting change. The Fifth Assembly of the WCC, in Nairobi, 1975, observed that churches had underestimated the fact that the struggle against oppression and injustice inevitably necessitates confrontations with powers and the handling of power. The JPSS was the framework in which these issues were then taken up.

In genuine efforts to change relationships between so-called donors and receivers (by setting up Round Tables and consortia), the power of money was mystified by talking about 'partnership' and 'sharing of resources'. The dominant role of money was underestimated in the actual practices of these alternative arrangements. Substantial progress was made in the theoretical and theological debate about mutual relationships, resource sharing and partnership. However, the obstacles faced in implementing good intentions were often not tackled in a straightforward way.

There was an early awareness in the ecumenical movement that development is not a linear catching-up process. Like theology, development has to be contextualized: there is no one development model that is applicable and valid in all parts of the world. It took a while before this early recognition of the need for contextual approaches led to serious attention being paid to the issue of culture and development. Likewise, the importance of spirituality as a sustaining force and the inspiring and motivating role of symbols has, at times, been underestimated (to be discovered again in the wake of the events of 11 September 2001, and reemphasized by the WCC delegation to the World Social Forum in January 2003). The issues of culture and spirituality are important, as 'development' in the South takes place in deeply religious contexts. The fact that the ecumenical movement, with its roots in religious convictions, can bring 'added value' in such contexts, was not sufficiently realized.

A New Situation

Since the WCC institutionalized its concern for development issues by establishing the CCPD in 1970, the world situation has changed considerably. The decolonization process – in the traditional sense of the word – has virtually been completed, the fall of the Berlin Wall symbolized the end of the Cold War, the process of globalization intensified, and the world is left with only one superpower.

The globalization of the world economy reduces the power of national governments to implement independent policies. Purely national approaches and instruments are becoming obsolete or even counter-productive. The world is witnessing a significant shift from classic (postwar) multilateralism to a more complex system of multi-layered global governance, in which national governments delegate or share competencies with local, regional, transnational and global bodies of both a public and a private nature. A fatal flaw at the heart of this newly emerging constellation is its lack of democratic credentials. To a large extent it remains highly unrepresentative of the world community and is characterized by deep inequalities of power and access to resources. While markets are globalizing, redistribution policies most definitely are not.

In a globalizing world, power is no longer solely organized and exercised on a local, national or international scale, but increasingly acquires a transnational, regional or even global dimension. The classical correspondence between the state, power and territory is being disrupted. Globalization has increased the demand for multilateral cooperation and the provision of global public goods such as financial stability, standard setting and environmental protection. The supremacy of nation-states over what occurs within their territories is increasingly compromised by the expanding jurisdiction of institutions of international governance and international law. This is not inherently bad, but it does affect the participation of citizens in decision-making processes which directly affect their lives. The territorially based concept of sovereignty is being replaced by a new regime with a power locus which is still diffuse. For many countries in the South this is nothing new, as they have for centuries experienced limits to their sovereignty. Other people have to get used to the fact that there are now effective constraints on state intervention and redistribution policies.

In compromising the principle of self-governance, globalization strikes at the essence of democracy, people's participation, and the concept of sustainable communities. This is not to glorify the concept of the nation-state or to elevate that model to the only possible way to build effective democracy and people's participation. The limits of that model have already become apparent in a world in which global warming connects the long-term fate of many Pacific Islands to the actions of tens of millions of private motorists across the globe. Effective control over crucial factors which directly affect the lives of the 'communities of fate' on the Pacific Islands lies well beyond the democratic reach of the people who are directly concerned.

At the same time, however, globalization has also inspired people to organize themselves and mobilize across national boundaries. The explosion of 'citizen diplomacy' constitutes the rudiments of a transnational civil society of which the WCC considers itself a part. However, not all the members of this transnational civil society are either 'civil' or representative. Also, considerable inequalities exist between the different members in terms of resources, influence and access to key centres of decision-making. In this respect, transnational civil society cannot be considered as truly representative of the world's people.

The most critical question to be asked about this emerging constellation of governance is governance of what, by whom, in whose interests, for what purposes, and guided by which ethical convictions? The ecumenical movement and the WCC have made important contributions to the United Nations system. They actively participated in the process which led to the Universal Declaration of Human Rights, reflected extensively about the crucial importance of people's participation, and have stimulated this wherever possible. They are now faced with the question of how to pursue their convictions in a globalizing world with diffuse systems of governance, and how to address anew the issue of political power that came to the fore in the ecumenical debate during the mid-1970s.

The two trends of a growing gap between rich and poor in many parts of the world, and ongoing environmental destruction, both of which accompany the process of globalization, are not new in themselves, but have acquired a new urgency. Economic deprivation and ecological degradation are often two sides of the same coin. There is an important link between environmental destruction on the one hand and poverty and inequity on the other. Poverty is often both a result and a cause of environmental degradation, and poor people suffer disproportionately. Poverty is a great polluter and so is over-consumption. The elimination of poverty, coupled with far-reaching changes in lifestyles and consumption patterns of the rich, are necessary for environmental protection. The traditional yardstick of the Gross National Product needs to be replaced by other indicators to measure the quality of life.

It has become increasingly clear that both these trends are a threat to peace and security. Protests against the results of indebtedness and misguided structural adjustment programmes have resulted in violence and have put fragile democracies in jeopardy. Conflicts about scarce natural resources like water are also likely to increase. Although poverty and inequity can probably not be considered as the main cause of international terrorism like that of 11 September 2001, these factors are likely to nurture anger and discontent. At any rate, this argument was used during the United Nations Conference on Financing for Development to advocate higher levels of ODA. It shows again that justice, peace/security, and environmental protection are closely linked.

In spite or perhaps as a result of increasing globalization, awareness of diversity and identity has also grown. This can lead to tensions and clashes between ethnic groups and can contribute to religious fundamentalism. It has also reopened the debate about the universal nature of human rights. Within the WCC it has stimulated fresh reflections about the kind of unity we seek and want to promote in view of the necessity to respect diversity and pluriformity. This debate not only has theoretical and theological implications, but also affects the methodology for ecumenical thought and action. The rise of religious fundamentalism and the events of 11 September 2001 have stimulated the WCC to be even more active in inter-religious dialogue.

Elements of a Future Agenda
These various developments require further reflection. They have implications for the agenda of the WCC and the ecumenical movement on issues which have long been referred to as development-related topics. Several steps have already been taken.

At its meeting in Harare, Zimbabwe, in 1998, the WCC Assembly – its highest body of authority – mandated the WCC to take up the challenge of globalization as a central part of the ecumenical agenda. It was emphasized that this work should build upon and strengthen existing initiatives by churches, ecumenical groups and social movements, support their cooperation, and encourage them to take action and form alliances with other partners in civil society working on issues pertinent to globalization. Globalization as a historic process has unfolded in different ways. Some, including indigenous peoples, regard economic globalization as a second wave of colonialism. Its most recent expression is driven by an exclusive focus on economic values. Unabated economic globalization radically disrupts communities, undermines spiritual values and threatens the ecological base of life. It concentrates power and wealth in the hands of a few.

Two years later the WCC Central Committee debated the issue of globalization again. It was observed that the logic of economic globalization is in opposition to the vision of the ecumenical movement of the unity of humankind and God's creation, the entire household of life. Lost is the understanding of the primacy of the dignity of the human person as made in the image of God, finding meaning in community. The underlying anthropology of economic globalization views human beings as individuals rather than as persons in community, as essentially competitive rather than cooperative, and as materialist at the exclusion of the spiritual. Economic globalization threatens the diversity of cultures. It has even affected churches, introducing a consumer-based religion and entrepreneurial style of ministry.[5]

The Central Committee made various recommendations:

- That member churches and the WCC should develop a comprehensive ecumenical theological analysis of economic globalization and its impact on the churches and on society, and provide a theological basis for the search for alternatives.
- That the WCC strengthen its capacity by involving representatives of churches affected by economic globalization, ecumenical organizations, social movements, research institutions and people with political and economic expertise in this area and maintain constant contacts. The WCC must contribute to developing a global response to the challenges of economic globalization that is rooted in local initiatives, so that its representatives can engage effectively at the global level.
- That the WCC focus on searching for alternatives to economic globalization based on Christian values in the following three areas: (1) the transformation of the current global market economy to embrace equity and values that reflect the teachings and examples of Christ; (2) the development of just trade; (3) the promotion of a just financial system, free of debt bondage, corrupt practices and excessive speculative profit making.
- That the WCC highlight economically instituted violence as part of the Decade to Overcome Violence. The WCC and member churches are encouraged to conduct studies on economic violence and to carry out advocacy in this field.

In the meantime, the WCC produced a number of dossiers on several aspects of globalization, criticizing the Washington Consensus and the 'pensée unique' and outlining an alternative vision. It also started a series of regional consultations on the topic, together with the World Alliance of Reformed Churches and the Conference of European Churches, and it established the Ecumenical Advocacy Alliance (EAA). The EAA, in which churches and church-related organizations participate, decided to focus its activities mainly on HIV/Aids and international trade.

In a document prepared for the United Nations Conference on Financing for Development, it is stated that an alternative approach to globalization is required that allows us to express 'development' and 'economy' in relation to our common vocation to live in right relationship with our neighbours, with the Earth and with our Creator. Such an approach includes a number of key affirmations:

- A recognition that real value cannot be expressed in monetary terms and that life – and that which is essential to sustain it – cannot be commodified.
- A belief in the inherent dignity of every person and a priority on creating the conditions for a dignified life.
- A commitment to an economy whose role is to serve the well-being of people and the health of the Earth.
- A focus on the ultimate aim of economic life to nurture sustainable, just and participatory communities.
- A vision of a global community whose interdependence is not reduced to trade and markets.
- An acknowledgement of a common destiny as co-inhabitants of the one Earth for which we all share responsibility and from which we should all equally benefit.
- A responsibility to uphold the right of all people – particularly the diverse communities of the poor and excluded – to participate in the economic, social and political decisions which affect them.[6]

This approach emphasizes again the need to reverse arguments: human beings and their communities should be the starting point, the goal and the means for social development. Obviously, such an approach necessitates thoughtful reflection about situations in which the interests of different communities clash. It should also be recognized that the various goals promoted under the holistic umbrella of JPIC can sometimes be in conflict. Here again, the question of how to deal with necessary trade-offs is important.

Broadly speaking, a distinction can be made between two contrasting approaches to the issue of development. One begins with economies and their growth and then qualifies this by saying that development has to be human, social or sustainable. People who follow this line could be called 'development qualifiers'. The other approach rejects this as a continuation of policies which have brought much harm to the world, and searches for a different path. People adhering to this position could be called 'development dissenters'. Both approaches exist in the WCC and the ecumenical movement. The debate will therefore continue.

NOTES

1 Richard D. N. Dickinson, 'Development', in the *Dictionary of the Ecumenical Movement*, WCC, 1991, pp. 268-74.

2 Jacques Blanc, 'Construire un monde solidaire. Une logique nouvelle, in *Les Bergers et les mages*, Paris, 1992, pp. 63-9.

3 Larry Rasmussen, 'Sustainable Development and Sustainable Community: Divergent Paths', in *Development Assessed: Ecumenical Reflections and Actions on Development*, WCC, 1995, pp. 163-81.

4 See the WCC background paper for the World Summit on Sustainable Development, 2002.

5   Quoted from 'Economic Globalization: A Critical View and an Alternative Vision', in Dossier 6 prepared by the Justice, Peace and Creation Team of the WCC, August 2001.

6   'Justice, the Heart of the Matter: An Ecumenical Approach to Financing for Development', prepared for the WCC by the Ecumenical Coalition for Economic Justice, a project of Canadian churches, January 2001.

3

The World Bank Mandate Today:
A Spiritual Interpretation

Alfredo Sfeir-Younis

There are many ways one could introduce and explain the nature and scope of institutional mandates, starting from activities that remain at the surface of one's true identity and proceeding to ones that are more subtle and interior to our institutional existence.

This is a very broad and complex theme. One starting complexity is that mandates and functions are always evolving and are subject to multiple interpretations. Even internally, there is always a debate on what the institutional mandate implies and how to interpret its various dimensions.

To say that the World Bank is a multifaceted institution is an underestimation. And, in this context, it is important to recognize that it is not always possible to rationalize all those aspects linked to the inner dynamics of human change: social, economic and other forms of change. It is not always possible to establish a clear assessment of cause and effect (i.e. the so-called separability of who causes what). Thus, to know who is actually ultimately responsible for the increase or decrease in the head counts of poor people, can take several years to discover. The same applies to most aspects of human transformation.

At the basis of this issue is the framework or development paradigm an institution or a country uses to address development challenges. In general, there are often three options available:

1   The most traditional and best known is the *material* paradigm.
2   What I call the *neo-spiritual* paradigm, where we retain the basis of the material paradigm and add some human or spiritual values – one example is so-called 'development with a human face'.
3   The *spiritual* paradigm, to which I will return, below.

As regards the World Bank, here are two very controversial statements:

1   Contrary to popular opinion, the Bank's mandate and development instruments have evolved rapidly in the last several decades. This evolution has been towards a more humanistic view of development. We are not just focusing on things, but on people and all actors involved. We have a more humanistic World Bank.
2   If 'self-realization' is the most essential ingredient in attaining the aims of our individual and collective spirituality, the Bank has been extremely instrumental in opening the necessary spaces for spiritual growth at all levels.

Evolution of the Mandate

Consider this fundamental proposition: the mandate has always evolved as a mirror image of the given ideology of development at any point in time.

Let me illustrate briefly. From 1945 to the 1960s, the Bank was fully involved in infrastructure development, as the 'take off' in developing countries was conceived as depending on physical and financial capital. Then, in the 1960s and 1970s, the Bank mirror image shifted towards poverty, assisting the rural and urban disadvantaged person, and so on. The result was a new rural development strategy to show that smallholder agriculture was the thing of the future. From the 1970s and 1980s and as a result of the energy crises of 1973 and 1979, the whole ideology shifted towards macro-economic stability and management. Adjustment operations were then in fashion and it was expected that international development agencies would generate the demanded liquidity in exchange for 'good policies'. The 1980s and 1990s witnessed a tremendous opening up to environmental and social agendas. It is here that the renewed concepts of *human development* and *sustainable development* found their ideological and political supports. Over the last few years the diversity in approaches and themes has increased and the inclusion of the poor and powerless has become increasingly important.

There are several reasons for the shifts outlined above. While Bank leadership has not been the only factor, some personalities have played an important role (e.g. Robert McNamara's Nairobi speech *Assault On Poverty*; Tom Clausen on co-financing and devising economic research; Barber Connable on gender, environment, etc.). Today, we owe most of the structural changes and the new course in our vision to James Wolfensohn, as the leader *par excellence*. Given world circumstances today (e.g. issues of human security, terrorism), it would be really interesting to know where the institutional mandate will go from now on. Have we exhausted all possible road maps?

The shifts in mandate described above will clearly go in the following directions:

1   People first as the subject and object of the development process – putting people first not as a matter of rhetoric but as a matter of human transformation at it best.

2   The resurgence of society's normative values and their influence in public policy making. These normative values are and will be playing a fundamental role in national and global policy, and institutional and operational activities.

3   Empowerment of the voiceless and the powerless: a major human revolution that makes explicit the who, where and what. This implies participation, a seat at the table, freedom of expression, and much more.

4   Being more explicit about 'who is who' in development. This would mean explicitly acknowledging indigenous peoples, Afro-descendents and all other minorities (e.g. colour, race, ethnicity, religion). There will be more transparency about the gainers and losers in development actions.

On the Mandate, Self-realization and Spirituality

The foundations of today's economic thinking within the Bank and in most development institutions are far from being spiritual. But our organization, in its mandate, concerns and actions, is not devoid of spirituality.

There are many elements to a spiritual paradigm, but one is essential: to be universal, so that everyone and everything is included. It is here that the World Bank is playing a fundamental role. In some cases, this role is very controversial, as countries themselves are not prepared to accept the principle of universality. Just think for a moment of the situation of indigenous peoples and minorities.

Another element is that of self-realization at the individual and collective levels. The Bank's empowerment agenda, its activities on participation and community-driven development, and its stands on gender equality, are just three examples where the World Bank creates the conditions for human self-realization at the collective level.

In presenting these issues it is important to distinguish different forms of self-realization. In the material paradigm, self-realization occurs, for example, through participation, ownership, empowerment, information, satisfaction of basic material needs, community-based approaches, access to justice, and much more. All of these material forms of self-realization have a spiritual dimension that must be understood. For example, in the case of empowerment one can go beyond political or economic empowerment and dwell in the realm of inner-empowerment. Thus, self-realization in the spiritual realm goes far beyond the above and enters into the realm of identity, fraternity, sharing, caring, love, inner-wisdom, the sacred, and so much more. In many ways, the World Bank has been instrumental in creating the material conditions for spiritual empowerment. Of course, it is not the role of the Bank to select instruments or impose patterns in this regard, particularly as the instrumentality in spiritual self-realization belongs to the very personal realm of individuals and their societies (e.g. yoga and meditation).

Experience demonstrates that it is essential to understand whether material self-realization leads to or is a necessary condition of spiritual self-realization. This is a very important and controversial matter. A safe answer is: not necessarily. In my view, by means of development, understood in a general sense, it is necessary to attain both forms of self-realization.

I advanced the importance of the concept of self-realization in a debate not long ago on the International Labour Organization's concept of 'Decent Work'. It is here where the differences between the two paradigms sharpen quite interestingly. For example, the debate on decent work from a material perspective would focus on good salaries and equal pay, safety, security, and the like. In the case of the spiritual paradigm, one would see decent work in terms of another space and the conditions for human self-realization in all aspects of life.

A change or evolution of mandate does not necessarily imply progress towards material and/or spiritual self-realization. The same is true in relation to the adoption of new concepts of development. In particular, even poverty eradication and environmental enhancement could be attained materially but at the expense of spiritual self-realization. Whenever there is a debate on mandates or economic development in general, the real question is whether one is working within the material paradigm or the spiritual paradigm. The answer to this question is not an easy one. One reason is that our immersion in one paradigm does not permit us to enter or criticize the other. Thus, the 'right answer' to this question leaves us with a dilemma conditioned by the ultimate choice of paradigm. The same applies to judging and assessing whether shifts in mandates are of the right kind or not, or whether the trajectory of socio-economic development is or is not appropriate. These are fundamental issues that need further elaboration.

What is the Mandate of the World Bank?
This question could be answered in many different ways and at different levels of sophistication. The Bank was created to reconstruct Europe and be a strong support for the Marshall Plan. However, Europe reconstructed itself faster than expected and the Bank moved into developing countries. Thus, the history of the Bank includes such projects as a railway project (France) and a water project (Spain).

If one were to define the Bank mandate at that time, one could say very simply that it was this: to assist LDCs in their socio-economic development. Within this context, economics and economic values always played an important role in defining our mandate (see the Bank's Articles of Agreement, for example). This is a crucial point that must be understood. The Bank was created as an economic development institution. It is in this domain that many development notions find their critical importance. Examples are economic growth, comparative advantage and economic efficiency.

In the beginning there were also lots of engineering and technical-feasibility types of work. Lately, the emphasis has changed and there is more work in the domain of the social, the environmental and even in the normative aspects of development.

If one looked at mandates in more subtle ways, one would see that the Bank does indeed embrace a large number of dimensions in relation to human welfare. In particular, its attention to poverty and its eradication has proved an essential focus, specifically on social and humanistic issues like participation, ownership, empowerment, etc. There is no doubt that NGOs, churches and the WCC have played a determining role in this respect. One must also recognize that there have been some important champions within the Bank who have moved the frontier of the new development agenda. Not only has the technical/engineering mandate evolved, but also the social and humanitarian mandate has developed.

As the Bank moves into the normative aspects of development, we also see important shifts in its normative work. Examples include justice system reform programmes, changes in the composition of bank lending, focusing on institutions for the poor, and empowerment. There is also increasing awareness of the role of value systems: on those values which form the foundation for what we do (e.g. corporate values (ethics) and development-related values like those involved in the Faith and Development Dialogue).

In a more material/operational sense, dimensions of our mandate are closely linked to the functions we perform; for example, the transfer of capital from rich to poor countries, the transfer of large sums of money to LDCs, and the transfer of knowledge and technology.

To all of this we need to add the role of the Bank as ombudsperson and regulator. This happens mostly in indirect ways, through issuing such policies as procurement. All these policies act as 'boundaries' in the policy dialogue with client countries.

It is also clear that the interpretation of the mandate is influenced by political ideology, politics and the world's circumstances. But this is something that every institution experiences. If it were otherwise, one would be working in a total vacuum.

The next major influence on our mandate, I believe, will be the ethical, normative, moral and spiritual values that are surfacing now. However, this 'battle' will be much more complex than the ones we are fighting on the economic, financial and institutional fronts.

What are the Successes and Failures in Terms of the Realization of Human Rights?

The general public and many organizations believe strongly that we do not do much about human rights, so that there are no successes and a great deal of negligence on our part. Others mistakenly judge us depending on whether or not we use the language of human rights. While some criticisms are valid, in the vast majority of cases they represent a distorted and very poor way to argue the case against the Bank.

In many ways, the manner in which we answer this question depends on our analytical framework. For instance, in presenting the Bank's achievements we used to adopt our own framework and ideology. This approach did not get us very far with NGOs and other advocacy groups.

In this realm of rights, there are many successes and we all know them: justice systems and access to justice by the poor; gender and land titling; indigenous peoples and land registration; Afro-descendents; Roma. The very controversial points are whether our programmes actually reach those whose rights are not being fulfilled and whether our macro framework for policies is a source of human rights violations. The position of our opponents is more ideological than empirical. Not that being ideological is wrong. We are all ideological!

There are many filters between what the Bank recommends and the final beneficiaries. Key filters are power structures; governance structures; executive, judiciary, and legislative authorities; access to institutions; and existing value systems.

Whether human rights are 'things' to add on or whether they form a new paradigm cannot be resolved here, but it is important to understand the implications as regards policy formulation and project design. Whether the neoclassical model has a built-in bias against the fulfilment of all human rights and the right to development is a fundamental question that will never have a definite answer.

What Major Issues Need To Be Resolved In Order To Eradicate Global Poverty, Increasing Inequality and Environmental Destruction?
The two options here are a radical departure from the paradigm of today or a move at the margin. The radical approach necessitates a new value system and a new institution. Is it feasible now? Other approaches, if properly managed, can yield some important results. Since this seems to me to be the situation we are facing right now, we will have to be very innovative in order to move in the desired direction. Here are a few suggestions:

- A major effort on issues of participation, community management and empowerment.
- Enhance collective action at all levels, including the global level. Churches, the WCC and NGOs are crucial, except when they replace local or traditional institutions.
- Recalibrate the role of governments.
- Establish a framework for the private sector.

To What Extent Do We See the Bank as Responsible and Accountable for the Results of its Policies?
This is a very tough question to answer because it may completely distort notions of responsibility, obligation, leadership and accountability. Also, it assumes that we own a process and the different situations within that process, and that we are vertically integrated – from the moment we recommend a policy until its final implementation. What level of accountability? The answer must be *both*: when policies are followed and when policies are not followed.

We are accountable to the Board of Governors and on everyday management to the Board of Executive Directors. They come from the executive branch of government. We assume that these governments are representative. If this representation is not legitimate, or perceived not to be legitimate, then there is a major problem. Should the Bank be accountable to the people? Given the institutional arrangements of today, it is very difficult to see how this form of accountability is possible.

Plans for the Future
The World Bank has begun a very deep, very profound debate on values and their role in development. It is a concerted and genuine effort to make sure countries are in the driver's seat. This is more than just a slogan, but it is extremely complex to put into practice. We are moving into other non-brick-and-mortar areas: social, environmental and ethnic, in particular. These are stimulating great controversy among donors and recipient countries in con-

nection with culture and development, faith dialogue, rights, corruption, and much more.

A mandate can be presented in writing, but its real test is when it confronts the reality of each of our client countries. One cannot apply a 'one size fits all' approach. The key point is to support the 'right' trajectory of change. We as Bank staff have only a minor role to play. Governments are in the driver's seat. Sometimes there is a 'breakdown' between the intent and the final outcome. Our main attention must be on the 'why' of the breakdown rather than on the mandate itself.

The roles of the material and spiritual paradigms cannot be disregarded. Often when we make our assessments we are simply using different paradigms or approaches. Even the books of the WCC and the many critics of our institutions perpetuate this confusion. This must be corrected.

Views and concepts of development are moving targets. Much more time is needed to debate the fundamentals.

4

The Evolving Role of the IMF and the Reduction of Poverty

Graham Hacche

The Constant Purposes and Evolving Role of the IMF

The Fund, like the Bank, was established as one of the institutions of global cooperation at the end of the Second World War, and after a period of destructive economic nationalism between the two world wars – a disastrous experience, which showed the problems that can arise for the world if countries pursue inward-looking, protectionist, 'beggar-my-neighbour' policies. This was an experience that should not be forgotten today when we deal with the challenges posed by globalization and open-economy policies that have brought prosperity to so many.

The Fund and Bank were born at a United Nations conference at Bretton Woods, New Hampshire, in July 1944. Forty-four countries were represented at the conference, and they drew up Articles of Agreement that defined the purposes and functions of the IMF. The Fund's purposes, set out in Article I, are exactly the same now as they were then. They are:

- First, to promote international monetary cooperation, exchange rate stability, and orderly exchange arrangements. (This refers, in particular, to the need to avoid beggar-my-neighbour currency devaluations harmful to other countries, which had occurred in the 1930s.)
- Second, to assist in the elimination of exchange restrictions which hamper the growth of world trade. (Again, this refers in part to the need to avoid beggar-my-neighbour restrictions on foreign exchange transactions. Note that this refers to restrictions on current account – mainly trade – transactions, not capital flows: the IMF's Articles explicitly allow controls on capital flows that do not restrict payments for current transactions.)
- Third, by facilitating the balanced growth of world trade, to help promote, as primary objectives of economic policy, high levels of employment and real income, as well as economic development.
- Fourth, to help member countries with balance of payments problems solve them 'without resorting to measures destructive of national or international prosperity', including the temporary provision by the Fund of financial assistance. As Article I puts it, the IMF's purpose in this respect is to 'give confidence to members by making the general resources of the Fund temporarily available to them under adequate safeguards, thus providing them with the opportunity to correct maladjustments in their balance of payments without resorting to measures destructive of national or international prosperity.'

These are still the statutory purposes of the IMF. And they have become increasingly vital over the past sixty years, not least because increasing international economic integration – globalization – has raised the importance of international economic cooperation. However, the work of the Fund today is quite different from its early years. In fact, the constancy of its purposes has required the Fund to evolve, because of changes in the structure of the world economy and the IMF's own membership, and also in response to lessons we have learned about economic policy.

Changes in the Structure of the World Economy since Bretton Woods
There are three main changes in the structure of the world economy:

1 The emergence and growth of independent developing countries. Of the 44 countries at the Bretton Woods Conference, fewer than 30 were from the developing world, and only 8 were from Africa, Asia and the Middle East combined. Today, there are 184 member countries virtually covering the globe, and 125 of them are developing countries, about 50 of them in Africa.

2 The increased international mobility of goods, capital and labour, and greater international integration of markets – which we call globalization. World trade growth has been roughly twice output growth on average in the postwar period. World trade as a percentage of world output, which fell in the interwar period, had by 1973 recovered to its level of 1913, and it has continued to rise since then. And there has been a vast increase in the scale of capital flows; they have been a vital source of finance for productive investment, although they have also been a source of financial and economic instability in some circumstances.

3 There has been the reintegration of formerly centrally planned economies into the world market economic system and into our institutions. Twenty-nine of our 184 member countries are counted as being in transition from central planning.

These changes have radically affected the work of the IMF. The influence has not just been one way, however: the second change, in particular, can be partly attributed to the work of the Fund, in promoting an open, multilateral system of trade and payments, and policies of adjustment and reform, which have contributed to the international integration of markets, and to the prosperity of the postwar period. The economic growth experienced in the postwar period is unprecedented in recorded history, and associated with this there has been a major decline in the proportion of the world's people living in poverty.[1]

Lessons about Economic Policy since Bretton Woods
The IMF's work has also evolved in response to lessons learned in the postwar period about economic policy.

First, especially during the period of inflation, there was stagflation, and increasing budgetary problems of the 1970s and 1980s led to an increased realization of the shortcomings and dangers of relying too much on short-term demand management policies, without a medium-term framework of fiscal discipline and monetary stability to anchor people's expectations and policy makers' plans. The need for a medium-term orientation in policy became clear.

Second, there was at roughly the same time an increased recognition of the importance of policies to attend to the supply side of an economy, as well as demand. It was realized that even for the most basic macro-economic objectives to be attained, macro-economic policies, which form the core of the IMF's work – fiscal or budgetary policies; monetary policies, which refer to interest rates and the expansion of money and credit; exchange rate policies; and other policies that affect demand in the economy as a whole – have to be supported by structural policies, which aim to improve the working of individual markets or sectors. This applies in the industrial countries; for example, it became impossible some years ago to argue that the chronic problem of unemployment in Europe could be solved simply by expanding demand. It applies also in the economies in transition and the developing countries, where distortions in financial and enterprise systems, as well as in labour and other markets, have made it impossible for macro-economic policies alone to attain desirable macro-economic outcomes – for economic growth, poverty reduction, unemployment and so on.

Third, there was in the 1980s and early 1990s an increased recognition in the IMF of the importance of economic growth as an objective of its own operations and policy advice. The IMF became more aware that the policy programmes supported by its loans would be inadequate if they aimed only for the correction of balance of payments problems: programmes also needed to establish the foundations for sustainable economic growth if they were to promote effectively the 'primary objectives' of high levels of employment and real income referred to in the Articles. I would add that the IMF has always emphasized that the kind of growth we promote is not growth in the size of economies for its own sake, but growth in real per capita incomes that increases human welfare and that is sustainable and equitable. Michel Camdessus, the IMF's managing director between January 1987 and February 2000, used to refer to this as 'high-quality growth'. It is the key to rising economic welfare and poverty reduction. There is no way of lifting the population of poor countries out of poverty, say on the scale that has actually been achieved in much of Asia in recent decades, without sustained economic growth. (This is not to say, however, that economic growth is all that is needed for poverty reduction.)

A fourth lesson: whatever the merits of exchange rate stability (an objective clearly stated in Article I) for a growth-oriented policy strategy, we have learned and relearned in a large number of currency crises how demanding are the requirements of maintaining pegged exchange rates, especially for countries open to the increasingly voluminous and agile flows of international capital. Such a crisis led to the collapse in the early 1970s of the global Bretton Woods system of fixed exchange rates, and subsequent crises have led to the more widespread adoption of flexible exchange rate regimes. Experience with currency crises has also highlighted the need for care in capital account liberalization. As I noted earlier, the IMF's Articles of Agreement allow restrictions on capital flows. Open capital markets were not seen as feasible at the end of the Second World War, in the context of a fixed exchange rate system and undeveloped capital markets in most countries: the danger was that with free capital flows, countries would suffer chronic financial instability, with governments losing any ability to influence monetary conditions, including interest rates. But with the collapse of the Bretton Woods exchange rate system, and with capital markets becoming deeper and more sophisticated, the benefits of capital account liberalization came more to the fore in the 1970s and 1980s. All industrial countries removed their restrictions on capital flows, and overall this has been a success: none of these countries has sought to reverse it. The IMF has viewed the liberalization of capital flows as a worthwhile objective for all countries because of the benefits they bring, but has emphasized the need for it to be done carefully and in an orderly way, when supporting policies and institutions are in place, to minimize the risks associated with volatile flows. It has never sought to make capital account liberalization an obligation of membership.

Fifthly and finally, in recent years we have learned to appreciate more the importance for the effectiveness of policy programmes, of national ownership of them: ownership not only by national governments, but also by the broader community, including civil society.

These lessons about policy – and there have, of course, been other lessons, and we are continuing to learn – together with the changes in the world economy mentioned above, help to explain how the Fund has adapted its methods and activities over the past half-century. In face of these developments, the Fund could not possibly have stood still and continued to serve its purposes effectively. There has been adaptation in each of the Fund's major lines of operation: surveillance, lending, and technical assistance.

IMF's Role in the Exchange Rate System, and IMF Surveillance

Up to the early 1970s, the Fund was regulator of the Bretton Woods system of fixed but adjustable exchange rates. After the collapse of that system, during 1971-3 – which was partly the result of growing capital flows – member countries became free to choose virtually any exchange rate regime: floating, pegged, etc. The Fund was given responsibility (in the Second Amendment of the Articles, which came into force in 1978) for exercising 'firm surveillance' over the exchange rate policies of members, which was to involve surveillance over all policies impinging on exchange rates. This was based on recognition that the key to exchange rate stability was provided by improvements in national policies that could be fostered by international cooperation, including the convergence of inflation rates at low levels, fiscal discipline, and structural policies to improve the efficient working of labour and other markets.

Surveillance is the central activity of the IMF. It applies to all member countries, year-in and year-out: every country has an obligation to subject its policies to the scrutiny of the international community represented in the

Fund. IMF surveillance gives the world community a voice in policy advice to each member country, with the aims of avoiding or correcting policies damaging to the country itself or other countries, and of promoting policies that support sustainable economic growth and financial stability. Surveillance takes several forms: country surveillance (which involves usually annual formal consultations with each member, and other contacts as needed); global surveillance (including global economic projections and analysis of the policies needed to improve the outlook); and regional surveillance. Note that it is the Executive Board, representing the entire membership of the Fund, not the IMF staff, that does surveillance; and that surveillance continues at ministerial level in the International Monetary and Financial Committee (IMFC), which meets twice a year.

In recent years, following crises in several emerging market countries, much attention has been paid to strengthening surveillance, including through more attention to exchange rates and financial sector soundness; the development of standards and codes of good practice in policy making; the promotion of transparency, etc. A major objective is crisis prevention. Strong, sustainable growth has also become a recognized objective of surveillance.

Surveillance touches on all policies that significantly affect economic performance and their international repercussions. However, as we reach areas at the margin of the IMF's mandate and expertise – which are in the macroeconomic/financial area – we rely increasingly on other institutions for assistance, particularly the World Bank. The current managing director, Horst Köhler, has emphasized, in particular, the need for the Fund to focus on its core responsibilities.

Finally, what has surveillance got to do with the reduction of poverty? First, financial and economic crises tend to hurt the poor disproportionately: crisis prevention is pro-poor policy. Second, high inflation hurts the poor, since they are the least able to defend themselves against it; and the IMF promotes low inflation. But the idea that the IMF is always, in all circumstances, trying to push inflation down is a fallacy. There are many examples of the Fund recommending that countries ease their monetary conditions – prominent recent examples have been in the IMF's advice to the European Central Bank and the Bank of Japan.[2] This advice reflects the Fund's promotion of policies that support sustainable economic growth, and this promotion of growth is a third way in which IMF surveillance helps the poor.

Financial Assistance

The changes in the world economy described above explain the shift in the Fund's lending operations, away from the industrial countries. No industrial country has borrowed from the Fund since the late 1970s, partly because of the increased availability for them of balance of payments financing from the world's greatly expanded private capital markets, and partly because of the preference of industrial countries for flexible exchange rates that can take the strain when pressures arise.

Meanwhile, the IMF's financing facilities have been adapted to the needs of other member countries. The needs of developing countries and countries in transition, and the recognition that the balance of payments problems they face can be addressed only in a medium-term context and through structural as well as macro-economic policies, led to the introduction of new facilities operating alongside the traditional 12-month stand-by arrangement requiring repayment within 3-5 years. Extended arrangements, introduced in 1974, provide financing for medium-term economic programmes, generally with disbursements over 3 years, with repayments over 4-10 years. The SAF (Structural Adjustment Facility) and ESAF (Extended Structural Adjustment Facility), created in 1986 and 1987, respectively, provided concessional loans to low-income countries – at 0.5 per cent annual interest – again to support medium-term growth-oriented adjustment programmes.

These adaptations – toward medium-term financing, on concessional terms for low-income countries – have been essential to enable the Fund to do its job of helping its developing country members address their balance of payments problems without adding to their already severe debt problems. They have been essential, in effect, to make the Fund relevant to these members.

The ESAF was enlarged in 1994, and replaced in 1999 by the PRGF (Poverty Reduction and Growth Facility). At one point Michel Camdessus suggested that this new facility be called AGAPE, which is the Greek word for brotherly love, and some thought was given to what this might be an acronym for (e.g. Accelerated Growth and Poverty Eradication Facility). However, it became PRGF to indicate that poverty reduction is the central objective, and that economic growth is recognized as the surest way of achieving it. The current managing director, Horst Köhler, has reaffirmed the importance of the IMF continuing to play its part actively in poverty reduction, although the World Bank has the lead institutional role. Also, in 1996, the HIPC (Heavily Indebted Poor Countries) Initiative was introduced to provide debt reduction, and it was enhanced in 1999.

How has the IMF been able to provide low-interest loans to its poorest members?

These are cheaper loans than could be provided from the IMF's 'general resources', which come from member countries' 'quotas' or capital subscriptions. The concessional facilities have been financed in two ways. First, from capital gains that the IMF has made on its gold holdings; but there have been limits to the extent to which the IMF's membership has been willing to agree to sales of the Fund's gold, because of its importance as a reserve and a basis for the Fund's financial strength and credibility. The second source of financing that has enabled the IMF to provide concessional loans is contributions and subsidies from its member countries. Thus, in the late 1980s, the ESAF Trust was created to support programmes of low-income developing countries designed 'to strengthen substantially and in a sustainable manner the balance of payments position and to foster growth'. There have also been contributions from member countries to help subsidize PRGF loans.

The IMF attaches conditions to its loans, not only to ensure that the IMF is repaid, so that its resources become available to be drawn by other member countries in need, but also to ensure that the borrowing country implements policies to resolve the problems that are at the root of its need for balance of payments support. The degree of conditionality attached to IMF loans to poor countries has varied.

Before the introduction of the SAF, so-called Trust Fund loans were subject only to limited conditionality (the establishment of balance of payments need and a commitment to efforts to correct the problem) with no performance criteria. Under the SAF, a Policy Framework Paper was drawn up for each country jointly with the World Bank. There were again no performance criteria. Under the ESAF, conditionality was made stronger than under the SAF, both because weak conditionality was viewed by the Fund as having been partly responsible for limited progress toward programme objectives under the SAF and because the financial contributions from member countries that made cheap loans possible could not have been raised without stronger safeguards. Thus semi-annual disbursements replaced the annual disbursements of the SAF, with performance criteria on both macro-economic and structural policies.

Under the PRGF there is more emphasis not only on poverty reduction as the central objective of policy, but also on country ownership of the policy strategy, including through broad public participation in the strategy's design. Programmes supported by the PRGF are based on comprehensive policy strategies set out in Poverty Reduction Strategy Papers (PRSPs). PRSPs are country-owned, each being prepared by the government of the country concerned in a participatory process involving domestic civil society organizations – including the poor – and external development partners. PRSPs are considered by the Boards of the IMF and World Bank for endorsement as the basis for concessional lending and debt relief. The targets and policy conditions in PRGF-supported policy programmes are drawn directly from the country's PRSP, but are focused on the Fund's core areas of responsibility and limited to measures that have a direct and critical relevance to the programme's macro-economic objectives.

Close to 80 low-income countries are eligible for PRGF assistance, and as of the end of July 2003, 39 countries' policy programmes were supported by PRGF arrangements, with loans outstanding amounting to $7.3 billion and undrawn balances of $3.8 billion. About 40 countries are eligible for debt relief under the HIPC Initiative, and as of the end of July 2003 the IMF had committed HIPC assistance of roughly $2.5 billion to 28 countries, of which $1.5 billion had been disbursed. For the countries benefiting from the HIPC Initiative, debt service payments are being reduced by about one half in relation to GDP, exports, and government fiscal revenue. And whereas before the HIPC Initiative eligible countries were on average spending slightly more on debt service than on health and education combined, all the countries benefiting from HIPC are now spending more on social services than debt service – on average almost four times as much; and all have shown marked increases in the share of health and education in their budgets under their recent IMF-supported programmes.

Technical Assistance

The third major activity of the IMF, after surveillance and financial assistance, is technical assistance. This consists of help for countries to strengthen their policy-making capacity – both advice on institutional organization and procedures, and the training of officials – and help with the design of particular policies, including reforms. Technical assistance, including training, in areas where the IMF has expertise, is a benefit of IMF membership, provided at no charge except for countries that can afford to reimburse the IMF.

Technical assistance became a formalized function of the IMF in the mid-1960s and grew steadily through the 1980s. In the early 1990s, requests for such assistance surged when countries in Central and Eastern Europe and the former Soviet Union began their shift from centrally planned to market economies. In recent years, the regional distribution of IMF technical assistance has gradually shifted from the transition economies to Africa, which now receives more than a quarter of the total. This is part of the increased efforts of the international community to reduce poverty in low-income countries, including helping countries to improve governance through capacity building.

The Millennium Development Goals and Monterrey Consensus

The IMF's instruments of surveillance, financial assistance and technical assistance are thus being applied today in all of the Fund's low-income member countries to the objective of poverty reduction. This objective has been made more specific by the Millennium Development Goals set out in the UN Millennium Declaration of September 2000. These goals, which grew out of agreements and resolutions of world conferences organized by the UN in the past decade, have been widely accepted as a framework for measuring development progress. They aim, in particular, to achieve a halving of world poverty by 2015, relative to 1990.

The goals were reaffirmed at the UN Conference on Financing for Development held in Monterrey, Mexico, in March 2002, where a two-pillar strategy for achieving the goals was endorsed by the international community. The first essential pillar recognized by the Monterrey Consensus is the responsibility and determination of low-income countries themselves to pursue sound policies and good governance. The second essential pillar is stronger international support for low-income countries' efforts. The managing director of the IMF has emphasized that 'the Monterrey Consensus is our framework for the development partnership'[3] and that the IMF is determined to play its full part in helping low-income countries establish and strengthen the first pillar, as well as in contributing to the second pillar, international support. However, the managing director has also emphasized that the advanced economies must do more, especially in living up to their pledges to meet the long-standing target for aid of 0.7 per cent of donor countries' GNP, and in improving market access for developing countries' exports and reducing trade-distorting subsidies, particularly for the agricultural sectors of advanced economies.

To conclude, there is no question that work aimed at the goal of poverty reduction in low-income countries is one of the IMF's main preoccupations. The IMF's role more broadly – in guarding macro-economic and financial stability, working to prevent financial crises, seeking ways of resolving more effectively the crises that do occur, and promoting durable and equitable growth in the world economy – is also, more than incidentally, pro-poor. No doubt the work of the IMF will evolve further in the years ahead as the needs of our member countries continue to develop and the Fund continues to learn new lessons from experience. For the foreseeable future, at least, it seems clear that the international community will continue to call on the IMF to do what it can for the poor, within its mandate.

NOTES

1   For example, the proportion of the world's population living on less than $1 a day (at 1993 prices) is estimated to have dropped from 55 percent in 1950 to 24 percent in 1992. See F. Bourguignon and C. Morrison, 'Inequality Among World Citizens, 1820-1992', *American Economic Review*, September 2002. The proportion has declined further in the past decade.

2   See, for example, the IMF's *World Economic Outlook*, April 2003.

3   Horst Köhler, 'Implementing the Monterrey Consensus', address at the High-Level Segment of the UN Economic and Social Council (ECOSOC), 30 June 30 2003.

5

The International Concept of Wealth Creation and Social Justice: A WCC Perspective

Pamela K. Brubaker

> The fundamental tenet of the current development model – 'progress, productivity, profits' – has brought with it the dispossession of the majority of the people, the desacralizing of nature, the destruction of the way of life of entire cultures, and the degradation of women.
>   Corinne Kumar-D'Souza, *Women, Violence, and Nonviolent Social Change*

> Although the WCC, World Bank and IMF share the common objective of poverty eradication based on values and ethics of life, 'The ecumenical community expressly rejects the neoliberal economic policies promoted by the World Bank and the IMF ... Far from reducing poverty or enhancing ecological sustainability, these policies have widened the gap between the wealthy and the poor, and have resulted in greater social exclusion and greater exploitation of the earth's resources ... By asserting justice, ecological sustainability and the creation of viable communities as our goals, the ecumenical community's emphasis differs from the dominant approach, which focuses on fostering economic growth ... For the ecumenical community, authentic human development can never be achieved when the ultimate goal is the amassing of wealth and material goods, creating an unquenchable thirst for more power, profits, and possessions.

These excerpts from the WCC paper 'Justice: The Heart of the Matter' succinctly describe the views of the ecumenical community on wealth creation and social justice. In this essay, I will elaborate the ecumenical critique of the neoliberal market ideology that informs the policies and practices of the international financial institutions and explore the ecumenical vision of just, sustainable communities, concluding with a discussion of pressing challenges.

Ecumenical Critique
The WCC has clearly and repeatedly stated in different venues that it rejects the neoliberal economic policies promoted by the World Bank and IMF.[1] The harmful effects of the Washington Consensus – liberalization, deregulation and privatization – on the world's people – particularly the poor – and the Earth itself are well documented. This form of economic globalization has led to increased inequality and environmental degradation. A study by Mattias Lundberg and Lyn Squire of the World Bank found that 'the poor are far more vulnerable to shifts in relative international prices, and this vulnerability is magnified by the country's openness to trade ... at least in the short term,

globalization appears to increase both poverty and inequality' (cited in Bello 2001: 239-40).

Activist Shalmali Guttal concluded in her study of globalization in Asia that biodiversity and environmental quality are threatened by export-oriented economic growth, which takes place through 'commercial harvesting of natural resources for value-added production and an increase in plantation and mono-cropping'. Privatization of land, water and resource rights is also a factor. These processes also alienate local communities – many of which are indigenous – from the resource base they depend upon and have in common. A report on neoliberal economic restructuring in ten African countries found that 'all too often policy decisions reinforce or aggravate existing inequalities… in many cases, economic restructuring has increased poverty and further marginalized women' (Brubaker 2001: 39).

The US Congress's Advisory Commission on International Financial Institutions, also known as the Meltzer Commission, supported many of the claims made by critics of the IMF and World Bank. Its report, issued early in 2000, concluded that instead of promoting economic growth, the IMF institutionalizes economic stagnation, and the World Bank is irrelevant rather than central to the goal of eliminating poverty (Bello 2001: 60). The Commission produced a number of devastating findings:

> Seventy per cent of the Bank's non-grant lending is concentrated in 11 countries, with 145 other member countries left to scramble for the remaining 30 per cent; 80 per cent of the Bank's resources are devoted not to the poorest developing countries but to the better off ones with positive credit ratings … the failure rate of bank projects is 65-70 per cent in the poorest countries and 55-60 per cent in all developing countries. (Bello 2001: 240-1)

Former World Bank chief economist Joseph Stiglitz has published articles and a book criticizing the policies of the IMF. He is particularly critical of the deregulation of capital markets, claiming it increases risk without increasing growth (Stiglitz 2000). In *Globalization and Its Discontents* (2002), Stiglitz charges that 'Ideology guided policy prescriptions and countries were expected to follow the IMF guidelines without debate'. Not only did these policies often produce poor results, but also 'they were anti-democratic'. Furthermore, 'those policies weren't questioned by many of the people in power in the IMF'.

These failures led both the World Bank and the IMF to declare a change in their policies to focus on both economic growth and poverty reduction. According to a 1999 statement from the Group of Seven finance ministers and Central Bank governors, a 'comprehensive development framework' replaced existing structural adjustment programmes. This new paradigm included the following elements (see Bello 2001: 50-1):

- Increased and more effective fiscal expenditures for poverty reduction, with better targeting of budgetary resources, especially on social priorities in basic education and health.
- Enhanced transparency, including monitoring and quality control over fiscal expenditures.

- Stronger country ownership of the reform and poverty reduction process and programmes, involving public participation.
- Stronger performance indicators that can be monitored for follow-through on poverty reduction.

At this time, the IMF established the Poverty Reduction and Growth Facility, which replaced the Enhanced Structural Adjustment Programmes. Any programmes supported by the PRGF are 'framed around comprehensive, country-owned Poverty Reduction Strategy Papers'. The IMF and World Bank cooperate in this endeavour, particularly on issues of conditionality.

The ecumenical community is not persuaded that these recent poverty eradication initiatives of the World Bank and IMF – although perhaps more in line with the Human Development consensus of growth with equity[2] – adequately break with neoliberal ideology and thus doubts their potential effectiveness. For instance, Jubilee 2000/USA – a broad coalition of religious and human rights groups – after reviewing the Poverty Reduction Strategy Paper process, concluded: 'the injustice that macro-economic reform conditions have not been subordinated to poverty reduction concerns is most disturbing'.

An examination of some recent IMF and World Bank documents and reports supports this charge. The IMF/World Bank *PRSP Sourcebook* states that following the 'principles of the Comprehensive Development Framework ... the objective is to encourage low-income countries to reduce poverty by focusing on a renewed growth-oriented strategy'.

> Economic growth is the single most important factor influencing poverty, and macro-economic stability is essential for high and sustainable rates of growth. Hence, macro-economic stability should be a key component of any poverty reduction strategy ... In most cases, sustained high rates of growth also depend upon key structural measures, such as regulatory reform, privatization, civil service reform, improved governance, trade liberalization, and banking sector reform.

The IMF Executive Board review of the Poverty Reduction and Growth Facility[3] in March of 2002 reported: 'Directors saw an increased focus on the sources of growth in the PRGF-supported programmes as being of particular importance'. They stressed the importance of incorporating structural reforms to develop the private sector, increase foreign direct investment, enhance external competitiveness, and increase labour productivity. The World Band Executive Board approved a Private Sector Development Strategy (PSDS) in February of 2002. The PSDS states: 'A significant part of the [World Bank Group's] existing work on policy reforms, such as that on privatization, competition policy, deregulation and strengthening of property rights, will help improve the investment climate in client countries.' A key prong of the PSDS is to more systematically attach conditions to future loans that are meant to 'improve the investment climate' in developing countries.

Two recent decisions by the Fund indicate that this mandate is trumping commitment to poverty reduction and country ownership of their PRSP. According to Inter-Press Service, the IMF has delayed Zambia's 1 billion dollars in debt relief until it sells its state-owned commercial bank. Nicaragua was told that it must privatize its vital water resources, despite legislation which would suspend any such plans without a national debate (Mekay 2002).

In his evaluation of PRGF strategies, David Tannenbaum (2002) notes that 'In the past, these reforms have translated into lower taxes on businesses that starve government of resources, labour law changes that weaken protections for workers, destabilized safety nets and lower wages'. The PSDS proposes to provide subsidies to the lower-income groups who will be negatively impacted by these policies. Yet, as Tannenbaum notes, 'The WB's own Development Report 2000/2001 points out that subsidies often do not make it to their intended recipients because of "leakage" or capture of the subsidies by richer groups'.

> Developing country citizens' ability to affect these policies is constrained by the power dynamics between the Bank and borrowing countries – with poor countries willing to accept Bank-imposed conditions as a *quid pro quo* for Bank approval to obtain new loans to pay off old debts and maintain a credit rating … Although the Bank favours involvement in policy formation by organized labour and other citizen groups, 'that's up to the countries' says the spokesperson. 'One person's civil society is another person's terrorist group. In some countries, dealing with labour unions may be anathema, but listening to consumer groups may be appropriate.' (Tannenbaum 2002)

Contrast this statement with the 'Good Practices for PRSP Design and Implementation' IDA and IMF document, which states: 'The PRSP process is designed to be open and participatory and to include all major stakeholders, including CSOs (even those which may be out of favour with the government)'.

A particularly disturbing example of privatization is IMF support for privatization of state-owned tobacco enterprises. The World Bank has identified tobacco use as an impediment to development. Its studies show 'that excise taxes work to reduce smoking rates and advance public health'. 'The Bank has also published important information on tobacco trade liberalization, finding that reduced tobacco tariffs and freer trade in tobacco products have dire consequences, raising smoking rates and increasing preventable death and disease.'

> The IMF has in many cases supported privatization of state-run tobacco companies, and has even supported reduction of tobacco excise taxes and tariffs – policies universally agreed among public health advocates to undermine public health goals … The IMF push for tobacco privatization is unswerving, and appears to be part of its ideological commitment to privatization. In several cases, the IMF has pushed for privatization despite intense local opposition. (White and Weissman 2002)

The World Bank and IMF claim many benefits accrue to developing countries from privatization and foreign direct investment. Technology transfer is one such benefit. In the paper 'Globalization: Threat or Opportunity' (2002), IMF staff contend: 'Information exchange is an integral, often overlooked aspect of globalization. For instance, fdi brings not only expansion of the physical capital stock, but also technical innovation.' However, as Stiglitz points out, the Uruguay Round of GATT strengthened intellectual property rights in an unbalanced way: 'it overwhelmingly reflected the interests and perspectives of the producers, as opposed to the users, whether in developed or developing countries' (Stiglitz 2002: 8). Walden Bello (2001) observes that a crucial factor in the industrialization of most late-industrializing countries, including the United States, is 'relatively free access to cutting-edge technology'. Yet this process of technological diffusion is now seen as 'piracy' by industrial leaders, such as the USA. Since TRIPs take the side of the latter, it makes 'industrialization by diffusion much more difficult. UNCTAD charges that this is "a premature strengthening of the intellectual property system ... that favours monopolistically controlled innovation over broad-based diffusion"' (Bello 2001: 19-20). Similar critiques could be made of other claims about the benefits of economic globalization.[4]

The success of IMF and World Bank efforts to focus on poverty reduction is also questionable. The *PRSP Sourcebook* points out:

> Growth associated with progressive distributional changes will have a greater impact on poverty than growth which leaves distribution unchanged. Hence, policies which improve the distribution of income and assets within a society, such as land tenure reform, pro-poor public expenditure, and measures to increase the poor's access to financial markets, will also form essential elements of a country's poverty reduction strategy.

However, a Staff Report from February 2002 noted countervailing measures to lessen the negative impact of growth policies on the poor in PRGF-supported programmes

> are not always accompanied by PSIA [poverty and social impact analysis], and even where it exists, the scope and depth of PSIA varies considerably across programmes. Most notably, the majority of the PRGF-supported programmes with important social impacts are covered neither by PSIA nor countervailing measures. (IMF Staff, 14 February 2002: 21)

The Structural Adjustment Participatory Review International Network (SAPRIN) found that little of their analysis 'made its way into country programming or back to Washington; none made its way into the Bank's own adjustments assessments, much less into adjustment operations themselves'. This is in spite of the fact that James Wolfensohn and the Bank, in engaging in SAPRIN, 'had acknowledged the critical importance of consultation, local knowledge, experience and analysis to the formulation of economic policies'.

The crucial challenge from the ecumenical community is to the neoliberal understanding of wealth creation primarily as economic growth. We ask: Wealth for whom? At what price? In its report from the World Summit on Sustainable Development, the WCC wrote:

> The underlying development paradigm, with its strong emphasis on economic growth and market expansion, has served first and foremost the interests of powerful economic players. It has further marginalized the poor sectors of society, simultaneously undermining their basic security in terms of access to land, water, food, employment, other basic services and a healthy environment. (*Echoes* 21/2002: 37)

Other analyses support these claims. For instance, a longitudinal study by independent researchers found that although there is some evidence that women's status overall tends to improve with economic development, economic growth can increase gender inequality (Forsythe, Korzeniewicz and Durant 2000). A recent UNICEF study found 'there is no fixed relationship between the annual reduction rate of the U5MR and the annual rate of growth in per capita GDP' (UNICEF 2002: 115).

The International Forum on Globalization starkly describes the vision that the embrace of 'unlimited expansion of trade and foreign investment' by the IMF and World Bank suggests:

> They consider the most advanced state of development to be one in which all productive assets are owned by foreign corporations producing for export; the currency that facilitates day-to-day transactions is borrowed from foreign banks; education and health services are operated by foreign corporations on a for-profit, fee-for-service basis; and almost everything that local people consume is imported. [Clearly, such policies] consolidate and serve the wealth and power of a small corporate elite. (IFG 2002: 52)

IFG member Walden Bello contends that the IMF and World Bank 'are to a great extent driven by the interests of key political and economic institutions in the Group of Seven countries – particularly in the case of the IMF, the US government and US financial interests' (Bello 2001: 60). Stiglitz (2002: xiv) makes similar claims about the IMF, also noting the cost of these policies: 'Inside the IMF it was simply assumed that whatever suffering occurred was a necessary part of the pain countries had to experience on the way to becoming a successful market economy, and that their measures would, in fact, reduce the pain the countries would have to face in the long run.' Although Stiglitz thinks that 'some pain was necessary', in his judgement 'the level of pain in developing countries created in the process of globalization and development as it has been guided by the IMF and international economic organizations has been far greater than necessary'.

Ecumenical Vision

The philosophy and vision of the ecumenical community differ radically from that of those actors and institutions that focus on fostering economic growth. In place of unlimited economic growth, it envisions sustainable human development based on a just, moral and caring economy. It believes that equity and human rights are central to poverty eradication; poverty is not just lack of monetary resources. Its vision is of a world filled with just, sustainable communities.

The WCC challenges the underlying anthropology of neoliberal economic globalization, which 'views humans as individuals rather than as persons in community, human beings as essentially competitive rather than cooperative, and human beings as materialist at the exclusion of the spiritual. Furthermore, economic globalization also threatens the diversity of cultures' (WCC Central Committee, 2001.) Instead, the ecumenical community offers 'an alternative way of life of community in diversity', grounded in a life-centred vision that affirms God's gift of life to all creation. Four essentials of this vision are:

1   participation: the optimal inclusion of all at every level;
2   equity: basic fairness that extends to all life forms;
3   accountability: 'the structuring of responsibility toward one another and the Earth itself';
4   sufficiency: a commitment to meet the basic needs of all life and to develop 'a quality of life that includes bread for all but is more than bread alone' (WCC, *Together on the Way*: 23).

This vision shares much with the people-centred consensus developed by the network of groups protesting against corporate- and finance-ruled globalization. The International Forum on Globalization claims 'the foundation of all real wealth' is 'common heritage resources'. These resources 'constitute a collective birthright of the whole species to be shared equitably among all'. It identifies three categories of common heritage resources:

> The first category includes the water, land, air, forests and fisheries on which everyone's life depends. The second includes the culture and knowledge that are collective creations of our species. Finally, more modern common resources are those public services that governments perform on behalf of all peoples to address such basic needs as public health, education, public safety, and social security, among others. [All these resources] are under tremendous strain as corporations seek to privatize and commodity them. (IFG 2002: 63-4)

For the WCC, a key policy objective is to finance, develop, manage and conserve these resources as 'global public goods'. Other key policies include promotion of just trade; regulation of financial markets to control speculation; and people-centred financing for development. Both the WCC and the IFG have detailed discussions of policies for a people-centred globalization, as well as of examples where these policies have worked.

The possibilities and limitations of income-generation policies and programmes for low-income people deserve critical scrutiny, as these have been supported by the IFIs and the WCC. Since the success of the Grameen Bank in Bangladesh in making small loans to poor women who used them to build income-generating projects that substantially improved their families' well-being, 'micro-credit' programmes like these are viewed by some as *the* solution to poverty. Grameen Bank founder Muhammad Yunus cautions that experience shows that unless the *poorest of the poor* are specifically targeted by these programmes, 'they will be excluded, as they are from almost every other opportunity'. He further cautions that micro credit alone will not empower the poor or lead to any significant drop in absolute poverty; other programmes, like girls' education and youth employment opportunities, are also necessary. His points resonate with the 'human capabilities' approach to development articulated by Amartya Sen and Martha Nussbaum, who argue 'poverty can be sensibly identified in terms of capability deprivation; the approach concentrates on deprivations that are *intrinsically* important (unlike low income, which is only *instrumentally* significant)' (Sen 1999: 87).

Income-generating projects can also increase the workload of women, which may already have intensified during periods of economic restructuring when crises in social reproduction are exacerbated. Economist Diane Elson argues that the intensification and extension of unpaid labour – what sociologist Saskia Sassen calls 'the feminization of survival' – is a hidden factor in many episodes of stabilization and structural adjustment. Unpaid labour can help absorb the shocks of adjustment since it replaces paid labour in the production of daily necessities, such as food and clothing. In her study of projects in Nepal, economist Katharine Rankin discovered that without development of collective consciousness of subordination, income-generating projects can perpetuate 'oppressive relations'. She contends 'micro finance demonstrates a clear gender dimension to this governmental function: here the transition from state-led to market-led approaches to poverty alleviation has been anchored to women's capacity to leverage social capital on behalf of the financial sustainability of formal lending institutions' (Rankin 2002: 17-18).

Another crisis in social reproduction is the 'globalization of mothering' – or global care chains – which arises in part from the 'care deficit' that has emerged in the wealthier countries as women enter the workforce, which *pulls* migrants from the Third World and post-communist nations to become caregiver, while poverty *pushes* them. In their introduction to *Global Woman: Nannies, Maids, and Sex Workers in the New Economy*, Barbara Ehrenreich and Arlie Hochschild argue: 'this trend toward global redivision of women's traditional work throws new light on the entire process of globalization'. It suggests 'a dependency of a particularly intimate kind … as affluent and middle-class families in the First World come to depend on migrants from poorer regions to provide childcare, homemaking, and sexual services'. This global relationship

> in some way mirrors the traditional relationship between the sexes. The First World takes on a role like that of the old-fashioned male in the family – pampered, entitled, unable to cook, clean, or find his socks. Poor countries take on a role like that of the traditional woman within the family – patient, nurturing and self-denying. This sexual division of labour feminists[5] critiqued when it was 'local' has now gone global, with 'inevitable trauma of children left behind'. (Ehrenreich and Hochschild 2003: 11-13)

The ecumenical community insists that debt forgiveness is essential to poverty eradication and building sustainable community. The WCC is very critical of debt relief programmes like HPIC, which are a means to achieve debt sustainability, not poverty eradication. Of particular concern is the new condition of HPIC-II that countries produce PRSPs. When I first learned about this, it brought to mind economist Mark Weisbrot's (1999) charge that the heart of the problem is that 'the dominant globalizing institutions are continuously altering the rules of the game so as to redistribute income and power upward'. Although the expressed concern of HPIC-II is to ensure that funds made available through debt relief go toward poverty reduction, the overall intent is to ensure that the loans are repaid. This benefits the corporate and financial elite at the expense of the world's many poor people. It inhibits any real redistribution of wealth.

The ecumenical community is demanding debt forgiveness for highly indebted poor countries and debt restructuring for middle-income indebted countries. The WCC wants a new just process of arbitration for international debt cancellation, one not dominated by creditors. The basis for these proposals is the biblical Sabbath-jubilee tradition, which offers a critical mandate for periodically overcoming structural injustice and poverty and for restoring right relationships. The jubilee is a recognition that, left to its normal and uninterrupted course, power becomes more and more concentrated in a few hands, and that without intervention every society slides into injustice. This tradition provides a strong basis for both debt relief and land reform.

The IMF addresses some of these concerns in its proposal for a Sovereign Debt Restructuring Mechanism (SDRM), considered at meetings in April 2003. Overall, the proposed mechanism is rather limited and does not begin to address the real needs of heavily indebted countries. But what is most telling is the response to the question of why countries shouldn't be allowed to use the SDRM to disqualify 'odious' debt, such as debt related to arms purchases or debt accumulated by previous non-democratic or corrupt regimes. First, the IMF asserts, 'one of the key principles underlying the SDRM is that any interference with contractual relations should be limited to those measures that are necessary to resolve the most important collective action problems'. Notice that the concern is for those who are to collect the payments, not those who must pay no matter what the cost. The document then claims that 'disqualifying "odious" debt would involve a radical change in the validity of creditor claims and the *sanctity of contracts*, which would have adverse implications for the operation of capital markets' (IMF, January 2003: D10; emphasis added).

This is the closest the IMF comes to using moral or religious language, at least in the documents I have read. In response to the claim that some debts are 'odious' – 'deserving hatred or repugnance', the IMF speaks of the 'sanctity of contracts'. *Webster's Collegiate Dictionary* gives two meanings for sanctity: '1: holiness of life and character; 2 (a) the quality or state of being holy or sacred; (b) pl., sacred objects, obligations, or rights.' And to what does the IMF apply this term? To contracts. This claim certainly lends support to charges that neoliberal ideology 'is the new religion of the market'.

This goes to the heart of the difference between the philosophies of the IMF – and perhaps the World Bank – and the ecumenical community. The international financial and trade institutions speak of property rights and the sanctity of contracts; the ecumenical community speaks of justice and human rights, the dignity of human life, and the sacredness of all creation. Now the IMF might also claim that it is concerned for justice, but it is the most limited form – *commutative* justice – which pertains to contracts and is based in civil law, or the relations of members of society to each other. (Even at this point, there are those who challenge the justice of existing debt.) The ecumenical community is concerned about *distributive* justice: the community's distribution of benefits and burdens – the whole in relation to parts, as well as social justice – the common good of the community.

The IMF and those who oppose debt cancellation make much of what they call 'moral hazard' as a basis for their position. (This is the argument that such action would encourage others to unfairly seek relief from their debts.) George Soros charges that 'the current campaign against moral hazard is just an excuse for resisting any kind of interference with the market mechanism. This resistance is based on the false doctrine of our age, namely that financial markets automatically tend towards equilibrium' (Soros 2000: 91). He argues, instead, for 'a level playing field'. The WCC elaborates on this idea of 'false doctrine' in describing the way 'the iron law of economics … assume religious status, justifying massive exclusion and sacrifice of human lives and nature in the name of economic growth through privatization and the liberalized and deregulated market' (WCC, 'Traps and Temptations').

Although the IMF seems to find the notion of bankruptcy for a sovereign nation repugnant, Jeffrey D. Sachs notes that Adam Smith favourably mentioned bankruptcy for sovereign borrowers in *The Wealth of Nations*. In a paper for the Brookings Institute, Sachs observes that there are two motivations for bankruptcy laws: overcoming collective action problems and offering a 'fresh start' to insolvent debtors. The first is based on efficiency, the second on both efficiency and equity (Sachs 2002: 1-2). Sachs contends:

> Any specific bankruptcy proposals launched in response to the IMF initiative should recognize the two intertwined motivations of bankruptcy: addressing the collective action problems and granting a fresh start … Repayments to creditors must be placed in the context of additional objectives: a fresh start for an insolvent sovereign, preservation of its public functions, and achievement of broad development objectives. (Ibid.: 4-5; emphasis added)

He is especially concerned about a fresh start for low-income countries, who 'have been stuck for two decades or more in a persistent debt trap from which they are not recovering'. For these countries, he suggests 'the basic standard for debt collection should be to restructure debts in order to provide a macroeconomic framework within which the countries can achieve the Millennium Development Goals' (ibid.: 27). Research by the New Economics Foundation shows that countries in Africa will *not* be able to meet these goals without much greater debt relief than that scheduled under HPIC-II (Greenhill and Blackmore 2002: 9).

Challenges

Our efforts to build just, sustainable communities face two great challenges: (1) how to ensure that economic growth is guided by values of social justice; and (2) how to correct the centrality of economic growth – particularly in the rich countries, which use a disproportionate and unfair share of the world's resources and contribute an excessive amount of pollution – so that global sustainability becomes reality. These challenges are interrelated. Developing a process that would prioritize social justice will likely require the support of those powerful groups, particularly in the wealthy countries, whose lifestyles are grossly inequitable. As David Hallman said in the WCC Report on WSSD:

> The countries and corporations which most benefit from the current economic model are also the ones that hold much of the power in international institutions such as at WSSD. They were not about to make commitments that would undermine their position of privilege and respond with urgency to global injustice and the ecological threats.

The necessity of linking socio-economic justice and ecological sustainability has been a recurring emphasis of the WCC (see, for instance, Santa Ana 1998; Goudzwaard and de Lange 1995). Yet the churches, particularly in the North, have been slow to respond to this challenge. David Korten addresses the relationship between the environment and basic needs when he develops criteria for the use of the Earth's resources. The appropriate concern is whether the available planetary resources are being used in ways that (1) meet the basic needs of all people, (2) maintain biodiversity, and (3) assure the sustained availability of comparable resource flows to future generations. Ethicist Timothy Gorringe suggests that if the standard of living enjoyed by the North cannot be generalized, then the issue of consumption has to be addressed by the wealthy nations. This is one of the most difficult challenges the ecumenical community faces.

Some Christians see this as not just a matter of ethics, but of faith itself – 'serve God or serve mammon'. Many thoughtful commentators believe the ecological crisis cannot be approached just as a technical problem; it is also a spiritual problem.

> The WCC's perspective is grounded in its conviction about the sacred nature of all Creation, and about life as an interplay of spiritual and physical dimensions. We uphold the common human vocation to live in right relationship with our neighbours, the Earth and the Creator, respecting the integrity of the Earth and working for the health and well-being of all members of the Earth community. Its sacred origin makes the Earth the common inheritance of all peoples for all times, to be enjoyed in just, loving and responsible relationships with one another. (*Echoes* 2002)

The WCC is holding regional consultations on economic globalization, which include representatives from other religions. They are finding common ground in a shared analysis and strategies for alternatives. These are among the efforts to develop the political will crucial to meeting these challenges.

Recognition and protection of human rights, particularly the second generation of social, economic and cultural rights, are one important way of trying to ensure that social justice guides economic growth. Sol Picciotto, who holds the Chair in Law at the University of Lancaster, writes:

> Increasingly, proposals are being put forward to constitutionalize the global public sphere by the introduction of human rights principles. These aim to provide a counterweight to globalization based on the neoliberal dynamic of the removal of barriers and the unleashing of the forces of economic self-interest, by introducing obligations of respect for human values.

He notes that, traditionally, human rights have been obligations on states; this is an effort to make human rights obligations on the activities of private actors, such as transnational corporations and international economic organizations (Picciotto 2001: 339). At the conclusion of its 25th meeting, the UN Subcommission on Human Rights resolved that the World Bank and IMF are bound by obligations enshrined in United Nations Human Rights Covenants and must incorporate them into the formulation and review of PRSPs.

Participation and accountability (enforceable human rights) are essential, but will not be fully adequate if global power imbalances are not rectified. Financial resources are needed for poverty reduction and ecological sustainability. Walden Bello (2001: 175) calls for an environmental Marshall Plan, with eco-friendly technology transfer. The IMF, World Bank and the ecumenical community call for rich countries to meet the UN target for development assistance of 0.7 per cent of GNP. The WCC and the movement for a people-centred globalization want this development fund to be controlled by the United Nations rather than the IFIs.

Conceptually, alternative ways to growth in GDP for measuring value and well-being could be useful in thinking about social justice and wealth creation. Such measures can help people rethink the meaning of wealth and poverty as being only about money. They can also have an impact on public policy and expenditures. Various people, such as Herman Daly and John Cobb, have developed alternative measures that are already being used. Some are questioning the rules for what counts as consumption rather than investment. Jeffrey Sachs (2002: 9) comments on the irony, given what we know about development, that education and healthcare are considered consumption rather than investment.

The work of Marilyn Waring has been groundbreaking, particularly in relation to the value of women's unpaid labour. She also shows the irrationality of how value is assigned. Dung, for instance, provides fertilizer, cooking fuel, and in some countries a basic building material for use in construction, maintenance and decoration. However, it is not included in a nation's livestock production accounts or energy production accounts. Waring adds: 'We also won't find the hours that women spend gathering, transporting, cooking with, processing, manufacturing, or decorating with it recorded as work.' But in Nepal the World Bank estimated that 8 million tons of dung are burned as fuel each year. As Waring says, this is a 'major instance of import substitution, and represents a national saving in terms of debt that would be incurred through the importation of commercial fuels if resourceful women had not processed the alternative' (IDRC Report 1997).

Although assigning value to unpaid labour can be a useful strategy for rendering it visible and impacting policy to improve the welfare of unpaid labourers, this is not the only viable approach. A WCC consultation in Fiji reported: 'Subsistence economy is still important for the life of the people and merits much more attention and support compared to the destructive effects of the monetarized economy and the spirit of competition that accompanies it.' One participant commented: 'People in the West understand that poor people are those who have no resources. But because our culture of communal sharing is so strong, for us the poor person is the one who has no family or friends' (WCC, 'The Island of Hope': 13, 18). Another approach is the development of local currencies and systems of barter, which brings the process of wealth creation back into the community. Just, sustainable communities will have a plurality of economies. Although the challenges we face are great, the vision of a world with enough for all motivates the ecumenical community to deepen its critique of neoliberalism and to struggle together on the way to that world.

NOTES

1   For example, at the UN Financing for Development Summit in March 2002 in Monterrey, and the World Summit on Sustainable Development in September 2002 in Johannesburg.

2   'The ecumenical community rejects models of financing for development that simply increase monetary wealth without eradicating poverty, and have no regard for how that wealth is generated or distributed. Models that focus on poverty reduction, long-term employment and environmental restoration contribute to growth as a by-product, not as an end in itself. In this respect, a "human development alternative", similar to that advocated by the UNDP, is much more in line with the goals of the ecumenical community' (*Echoes* 2002). 'Attacking poverty directly – as a matter of human rights, to accelerate development and to reduce inequality within and among nations – has become an urgent global priority' (UNFPA 2002: 5).

3   'IMF Executive Board Reviews the Poverty Reduction and Growth Facility', Public Information Notice (PIN) no. 02/30, 15 March 2002. This was a required two-year review of PRGF, scheduled when the initiative was adopted. The Executive Board claims growth is critical for achieving poverty reduction and attention to the sources of growth is essential in developing appropriate policies and projections. (A fact sheet on IMF Conditionality dated 4 December 2002 also included price and trade liberalization in a list of policies which 'address structural impediments to healthy growth'.) This emphasis on growth is in part a response to a primary criticism that the IMF structural adjustment programmes caused economic stagnation.

4   For instance, Susan George points out that foreign direct investment 'consists mostly of mergers and acquisitions that result in harmful economic concentration and job losses, and in any case such investment flows to only a dozen or so countries'. See 'Another World is Possible', *Echoes* 21/2002: 9. For an exhaustive overview, see the Structural Adjustment Participatory Review International Network (SAPRIN), 'The Policy Roots of Economic Crisis and Poverty: A Multi-Country Assessment of Structural Adjustment,' April 2002.

5   Several major World Bank reports provide strong empirical evidence that the gender-based division of labour and the inequalities to which it gives rise tend to slow development, economic growth and poverty reduction. Gender inequalities often lower the productivity of labour, in both the short term and the long term, and create inefficiencies in labour allocation in households and the general economy. They also contribute to poverty and reduce human well-being.

REFERENCES

Bello, Walden, *The Future in the Balance: Essays on Globalization and Resistance*, Food First Books, 2001.

Brubaker, Pamela K., *Globalization at What Price? Economic Change and Daily Life*, Pilgrim Press, 2001.

Echoes: Justice, Peace and Creation News 21/2002, Special Issue on Global Economic Justice.

Ehrenreich, Barbara and Arlie Russell Hochschild (eds), *Global Woman: Nannies, Maids, and Sex Workers in the New Economy*, Metropolitan Books, 2003.

Elson, Diane, 'Talking to the Boys: Gender and Economic Growth Models,' in *Feminist Visions of Development*, Routledge, 1998, 155-70.

Forsythe, Nancy, Roberto Patricio Korzeniewicz, and Valerie Durant, 'Gender Inequalities and Economic Growth: A Longitudinal Evaluation,' *Economic Development and Cultural Change* 48, no. 3 (April 2000): 573-617.

Gnanadason, Aruna, Musimbi Kanyoro, and Lucia Ann McSpadden (eds), *Women, Violence, and Nonviolent Social Change*, Geneva: WCC Publications, 1996.

Goudzwaard, Bob and Harry de Lange, *Beyond Poverty and Affluence: Toward an Economy of Care*, WCC Publications and Eerdmans, 1995; first published in the Netherlands in 1986.

Greenhill, Romilly and Sasha Blackmore, 'Relief Works: African Proposals for Debt Cancellation – and Why Debt Relief Works', Report from Jubilee Research at the New Economics Foundation, August 2002, http://www.jubileeresearch,org.

Hallman, David, 'Report on the World Summit on Sustainable Development', accessed at http://www.wcc-coe/org/wcc/what/jpc/wssd-report.html.

IDA and IMF, 'Good Practices for PRSP Design and Implementation: A Summary for Practitioners', 3.

Internationalization Forum on Globalization, *Alternatives to Economic Globalization: A Better World Is Possible*, Berrett-Koehler Publishers, 2002.

IMF, 'The Design of the Sovereign Debt Restructuring Mechanism – Further Considerations', 27 November 2002.

IMF, 'Proposals for a Sovereign Debt Restructuring Mechanism (SDRM): A Factsheet', January 2003.

'IMF Board Discusses Possible Features of A Sovereign Debt Restructuring Mechanism', *Public Information Notice* (PIN) no. 03/06, 7 January 2003.

IMF Staff, 'Globalization: Threat or Opportunity?' Issue Brief 00/01, 12 April 2000, corrected January 2002.

IMF Staff, 'Review of the Poverty Reduction and Growth Facility: Issues and Options,' 14 February 2002: 21.

International Development Research Centre, 'IRDC Report', 9 May 1997.

Jubilee 2000/USA, 'End of the Year Statement', 2000.

Macan-Markar, Marwaan, 'Labour-Rights: South Korea Leads in Putting Value in Women's Work', *Inter- Press Service*, 25 October 2001.

Mekay, Emad, 'IMF Strong-Arming Debtors Despite New Lending Guidelines', *Inter-Press Service*, 10 December 2002.

North-South Institute, 'Putting a Value on Unpaid Work', *North-South Institute Newsletter* vol. E, no. 2 (1999).

Nussbaum, Martha, *Women and Human Development: The Capabilities Approach*, Cambridge University Press, 2000.

Picciotto, Sol, 'Democratizing Globalization', in Daniele Drache (ed.), *The Market or the Public Domain: Global Governance and the Asymmetry of Power*, Routledge, 2001, 335-59.

Raddon, Mary-Beth, 'Community Currencies, Value and Feminist Economic Transformation', *Women and Environments International Magazine* no. 54/55 (spring 2002), 24-6.

Rankin, Katherine N., 'Social Capital, Microfinance, and the Politics of Development', *Journal of Feminist Economics* 8 (1), 2002, 1-24.

Sachs, Jeffrey D., 'Resolving the Debt Crisis of Low-Income Countries', *Brookings Papers on Economic Activity*, 1: 2002.

Santa Ana, Julio, *Sustainability and Globalization*, WCC Publications, 1998.

Sen, Amartya, *Development as Freedom*, Alfred A. Knopf, 1999.

Soros, George, 'The New Global Financial Architecture', in Will Hutton and Anthony Giddens (eds), *Global Capitalism*, New York: New Press, 2000, 86-92.

Stiglitz, Joseph E., 'The Insider', *The New Republic* 222, nos. 16-17 (17-24 April 2000), 56-60.

Stiglitz, Joseph E., *Globalization and Its Discontents*, W. W. Norton, 2002.

Structural Adjustment Participatory Review International Network (SAPRIN), 'The Policy Roots of Economic Crisis and Poverty: A Multi-Country Assessment of Structural Adjustment', April 2002.

Tannenbaum, David, 'Obsessed: The Latest Chapter in the World Bank's Privatization Plans', *Multinational Monitor*, September 2002, 9-12.

UNFPA, *State of World Population 2002*, United Nations Publications, 2003.

UNICEF, *The State of the World's Children 2003*, United Nations Publications, 2002.

WCC, 'The Island of Hope: An Alternative to Economic Globalization', 2001.

WCC, 'Justice: The Heart of the Matter: An Ecumenical Approach to Financing for Development, January 2000'. Paper prepared for the WCC by the Ecumenical Coalition for Economic Justice, a project of Canadian churches.

WCC, 'Report of the Policy Reference Committee II (Adopted) WCC Central Committee, 2001.

WCC on Summit on Sustainable Development, Echoes 21/2002 (37).

WCC, 'There Are Alternatives to Globalization', 2000.

WCC, *Together on the Way, Report from the Eighth Assembly, Harare, Zimbabwe, December 1998*, available at www.wcc-coe.org.

WCC, 'Traps and Temptations', in *Lead Us Not into Temptation: Churches' Response to the Policies of International Financial Institutions*.

Weisbrot, Mark, *Globalization*, Center for Economic and Policy Research, 1999.

White, Anna and Robert Weissman, 'The Hand-Off to Big Tobacco: IMF Support for Privatization of State-Owned Tobacco Enterprises', *Multinational Monitor*, September 2002, 13-17.

World Bank, *Integrating Gender into the World Bank's Work*, 2002.

World Bank, *Overview of Poverty Reduction Strategies*, last updated 11/21/2002.

World Bank, *Poverty Reduction Strategy Sourcebook*, accessed 1/26/2003.

World Bank, *Private Sector Development Strategy – Directions for the World Bank Group*, n.d.

6

Wealth Creation and Social Justice: An IMF Perspective

Peter S. Heller

Over the last decade the IMF has moved forcefully to integrate issues of poverty reduction into the mainstream of its policy objectives in fostering growth and employment creation. This essay examines the Fund's perspective on the promotion of poverty reduction and improved distributional incomes. It examines the relative balance that must be sought between strictly growth-enhancing policies and those policies that are specifically targeted at poverty reduction and equity. It also explores how issues of social justice and environmental sustainability are taken into account by the Fund in working with its member countries.

In order to assess the extent to which wealth creation may coexist with the occurrence of absolute and relative poverty, it is useful to describe how issues of poverty and income distribution relate to the Fund's central mandate.

It is helpful to start by emphasizing the objectives of the IMF as derived from its Articles of Agreement: 'to contribute to the promotion of high levels of employment and real income and to the development of the productive resources of all members as primary objectives of economic policy'. The Fund's understanding of this statement of purposes has evolved considerably over time, taking account of the views of its shareholders. Specifically, there is now recognition of the importance of poverty reduction as an equally critical objective in its own right, side by side with economic growth.

Growth is seen as necessary for poverty reduction, but poverty reduction is recognized as a factor contributing to the achievement of high-quality growth. The new approach of the Fund and the World Bank 'recognizes the increasing evidence that entrenched poverty and severe inequality in economic opportunities and asset endowments can themselves be impediments to growth'.[1] Most important, the Fund has recognized that extreme poverty among the poorest nations of the world cannot be tolerated, but must be forcefully addressed. In his speech to the Monterrey Conference, the managing director, Horst Köhler, emphasized the importance of efforts to overcome world poverty.[2]

Equity issues are also pertinent. The Fund has come to recognize that growth in the context of high income inequality is not likely to have a large impact on poverty reduction. Furthermore, improvements in income distribution are likely to be an important instrument for the achievement of economic growth. At the time of the IMF's 50th anniversary, the managing director, Michel Camdessus, explicitly emphasized the importance of policies to improve income distribution and the implications for IMF operations of such a concern. He suggested that public support for a sustained course of adjustment and reform is most likely when 'the distribution of income and opportunities to attain economic advancement are seen as relatively fair or at least not outrageously biased toward privileged groups'. Moreover, he described the various channels – economic, political and social – through which improvements in income distribution may positively affect the growth process and a distributional content. As such, while noting that income distributional issues are not the central mandate of the IMF, he emphasized that 'the IMF cannot but call the attention of the country and the IMF membership to income inequality and its potential adverse consequences for the social fabric and sustainable growth'. Thus, redistributive policies, particularly expenditure policies, are widely recognized and supported as a way to improve the income distribution in member countries.

In judging the policies necessary to achieve poverty reduction and real economic growth, it is vital to come to grips with the sources of growth, the causes of persistent poverty, and the factors associated with successful poverty reduction efforts. While much is known, the economics profession still has much to learn about these issues. The Fund seeks to be up to date with the academic literature as well as with lessons drawn from experience. It relies heavily on the World Bank, given its long-standing work on these issues.

Finally, a critical element of the Fund's approach to these issues is that policies should be country-driven. Lending to low-income countries should be conditional on poverty-reduction strategies drafted by the countries themselves, which are grounded in a country's own assessment of the causes and dynamics of poverty.

What does the IMF see as the possibilities and limits of the process of so-called wealth creation in solving the poverty problem? Wealth creation can be narrowly defined in terms of income generation or more broadly as the creation of assets, both in terms of physical and human capital. 'Poverty', of course, is a multi-dimensional concept, relating not only to a low absolute income level but also to various indicators that define an unsatisfactory level of welfare (poor sanitation or access to clean water, high exposure to disease and premature mortality, illiteracy, etc.). In terms of its poverty reduction efforts, the Fund's principal focus is related to issues of absolute poverty, recognizing that *relative* poverty may exist even in the most developed of nations.

As indicated above, the IMF – and the economics profession more generally – has come to believe that the evidence forcefully argues that wealth creation – manifested by real economic growth in incomes and employment – is the principal and most forceful engine by which poverty is reduced. Substantial evidence has accumulated over the last two decades to demonstrate this. Growth in income is generally associated with an increase in a country's stock of physical and human capital though, as discussed below, in situations of high inequality, the assets of the poor may not grow commensurately.

Other important factors influence the extent to which growth has an impact on poverty reduction. Growth can occur nationally, but poor regions may experience less growth or may benefit less in terms of poverty reduction as a result of a given national rate of growth. Specific government programmes may be necessary to ensure that the poor do benefit in terms of new jobs or in the receipt of key social services critical to the accumulation of human capital.

Moreover, as noted above, multiple aspects of poverty must be recognized. Even if real income growth contributes to reduced poverty (in terms of the number of households below some income cut-off point), it may not have as significant an impact on other indicators of poverty.

Macro-economic stability is critical, both for fostering rapid growth and sustained poverty reduction. Periods of macro-economic instability can result in greater inequality (as the rich are more capable of protecting their assets in such situations), prove more harmful to the poor, and may result in the *creation* of more poor, as non-poor fall below the poverty line in periods of crisis. Moreover, in periods of macro-economic instability, the pressures for budgetary retrenchment often affect the poor most. Even with the best intentions with respect to social safety-net programmes and policies to shield expenditures on vital social services, it may be difficult to avoid cutbacks in some areas that affect the poor.

The evidence also suggests that wealth creation results in 'churning' in the poverty status of households. Inevitably, in the process of real growth, some groups and sectors benefit, while others lose out. In net terms, poverty rates may decline but some households may become poor at the same time that others escape poverty.

Finally, real economic growth in terms of incomes may also occur at the expense of a depletion of a country's natural resource base, so that *net* wealth creation may be lower than would be implied by the growth in gross capital assets. Sustainability should thus be an important criterion for assessing the quality of a country's economic growth process.

Is it growth alone, or rather growth plus distribution, that can eliminate poverty? The key issue is how to improve the poverty reduction elasticity of growth. Specifically, how to ensure that growth has a significant impact on poverty reduction? While there is much empirical evidence that demonstrates that economic growth reduces poverty rates – the Asian experience of the last several decades illustrates this – it is also clear that growth alone does not eliminate absolute poverty in some contexts. In situations of high inequality (say, in Latin America), one can observe significant growth in real incomes while many still remain in absolute poverty. And, of course, in terms of relative poverty, even the wealthiest countries of the world continue to demonstrate significant rates of poverty.

Devising and implementing strategies for growth that are particularly poverty reducing is not easy or always obvious by any means. In his last speech as managing director, Michel Camdessus emphasized the importance of pursuing high-quality growth: growth that can be sustained over time without engendering macro-economic imbalances; growth that fosters human capital development; growth that is based on a continuous effort at promoting greater equity, poverty alleviation, and empowerment of the poor; and growth that promotes protection of the environment and respect for national cultural values.[3]

Redistributional policies are thus of critical importance in 'reducing' poverty or at least alleviating some of its most adverse effects, particularly when income inequality is severe. The challenge is to pursue a course that both sustains high growth and provides for redistribution. This requires efforts to minimize the adverse efficiency effects that can arise when there is too forceful a concentration on redistribution (e.g. from excessively high marginal tax rates, untargeted subsidies, or price controls).

Redistributional efforts can take several forms. The public sector, in its expenditure policies, can subsidize the provision of basic social services – in education and health – which contribute not only to the current welfare of the poor but also to the accumulation of human capital in younger generations of the poor so that they have the potential to escape poverty.

Equally, the government, through specific targeted subsidy and transfer policies, can seek to augment, directly or indirectly, consumption of the poorest groups. Public works schemes may also be provided to supplement incomes, particularly for the unemployed. Policies are needed to enable the poor, particularly in rural areas, to reduce their vulnerability to risk.

During periods of macro-economic instability, social safety-net programmes may provide assistance to non-poor that have fallen into poverty (see below). They serve both as a mechanism to generate income transfers to the poor and also as a mechanism for investment in human capital that can prevent the adverse long-term effects that macro-economic shocks can have on poor households. Social 'safety-rope' policies – such as unemployment insurance – can prevent poverty from being experienced by non-poor individuals facing shocks which might come from macro-economic instability or from wealth creation itself.

Moreover, even if the focus is only on growth without redistributional efforts, there is increasingly a recognition that the *kinds* of policies used to promote growth must take account of the objective of poverty reduction. This may affect the kinds of investment policies pursued or the focus of public expenditure. It may also influence the posture taken by macro-economic policy makers in relation to the relative weight to be placed on real growth and inflation. Accepting a higher inflow of foreign assistance may create some macro-economic risks which may be deemed acceptable in view of the objective of poverty reduction. In other words, macro policies need mutually to support the realization of both growth and poverty reduction goals.

Does the Fund acknowledge that poverty is also induced by, or grows, during such a process? What place do we give to income generation by the poor themselves? As noted above, there is no question that some individuals or households may fall into poverty in the context of the normal growth process. But the evidence suggests that the net number in poverty will fall with growth. The key issue is to put in place public policies that help those employed in declining sectors to move on to growing sectors, while cushioning the adverse effects experienced by those left short in the process.

A very high emphasis should be placed on income generation by people in poverty themselves, as well as on the need to create opportunities for future high-value employment by the children of today's poor. That is why so much effort has gone into studying the factors underlying poverty among poor households and understanding the kinds of policy instruments that can reach and target income generation by the poor. Policies that specifically target income creation opportunities for the poor have included micro-credit schemes, public works for the unemployed, and the provision of training and agricultural extension. Of course, education and health programmes seek to build up the human capital of poor children in order to enhance their capacity for productive employment in the future. Creating jobs for the *non-poor* is also important and relevant for poverty reduction policies, enhancing overall growth and stimulating demand in ways that can generate incomes for the poor.

However, it is also important to recognize that some groups of the poor may not be able to rise above poverty through their own efforts and that targeted forms of income or consumption assistance may be vital as a result to alleviate the consequences of poverty.

Finally, the Bank and the Fund have emphasized the importance of the participation by the poor in terms of the formulation of strategies for poverty reduction in a country. Such an approach is integral to achieving meaningful country ownership of such strategies.

How does the Fund seek to ensure that economic growth is guided by the values of social justice? 'Social justice' is obviously a very normative term. Even defining it may provoke controversy, for example as to whether it should include issues of race, gender or income. Each country, by its culture, religion(s) or history, may define social justice quite differently. President Bush's concept of 'compassionate conservatism' is certainly different from the concept of social justice espoused by many European governments. Even across segments of the Christian church, the concept of social justice and the tools to achieve it may differ. Thus, what constitutes a 'fair' or 'just' income distribution may not be readily accepted by all countries.

Yet there may be some commonality in defining core elements of social and ethical justice. Some would argue that there are inalienable human rights that are transcendent across cultures and religions. For example, note the Declaration Toward a Global Ethic, which was approved by the Parliament of the World's Religions in Chicago in 1993. In some ways, the definition of the Millennium Development Goals can also be construed as asserting such rights, in effect recognizing the elements of what makes for a fair and just society. Indeed, Horst Köhler has argued forcefully that 'cultural and religious diversity… enriches this planet'.[4] He has emphasized the importance of building 'bridges through dialogue, cooperation, and inclusion, to create a sense of global ethics… and a respect for human rights'.

The emphasis of the IMF and the World Bank on country-led strategies for poverty reduction reflects the recognition that the people of countries themselves must define and own how to go about reducing poverty and where the key priorities for poverty reduction strategies should be, thus allowing for cultural and religious diversity. Social justice is far better achieved when those directly concerned reveal and put their own values in place.

An important element of the new approach of the Bank and the IMF in their poverty reduction efforts is the effort to conduct poverty and social impact analyses (PSIAs). In low-income countries, the IMF is promoting the use of such analyses to facilitate, *ex ante*, the assessment of the distributional impact of policies and thus the improvement of policies at the *design* stage, including the minimization, *ex ante*, of adverse effects. In this respect the IMF, along with other development partners, is working toward an understanding of the social impact of key policy interventions before, during and after they are implemented, so that the trade-offs of policy choices can be fully understood and planned for.

Alleviating the worst manifestations, in welfare terms, of poverty is thus critical *before* safety nets are considered. The principal emphasis should be on pursuing policies that foster economic growth and opportunities for income generation and that provide critical health and education services to promote human capital development As indicated above, policies that foster macro-economic stability as well as the dynamics of poverty generation in the future are integral to any long-term success.

This is not to deny the importance of safety nets, but they are not sufficient for a comprehensive poverty reduction strategy. While important, their emphasis is to limit the extent to which policy reforms or macro-economic adjustment measures have an adverse impact on the welfare of the poor and provide a welfare cushion for non-poor households who fall into poverty. Safety nets, when used, need to be tailored to the specific country setting.

Moreover, as clearly argued by Horst Köhler at the time of the Monterrey Conference, the burden of poverty reduction efforts is not solely a problem of the poorest countries. The broader international community has an important responsibility as well, in terms of fostering a global macro-economic environment supportive of economic growth; in opening up the markets of industrial and emerging market countries to the exports of developing countries; in promoting the provision of global public goods; in providing increased financial assistance to the poorest countries; in resolving financial crises in countries that can threaten the global economy; and in attacking the sources of climate change, which affects the poorest countries far more than the rich.

Growth and sustainability of the environment are at least partially contradictory objectives. How can the concept of and the striving for economic growth (especially in the rich countries) take place in a way that also facilitates global sustainability? This poses important but difficult issues. The international community has recognized, in the context of the Kyoto Accord and in the various reports of the Third Intergovernmental Panel on Climate Change, that as a starting point, rich countries must introduce mitigation strategies to reduce the rate of emission of global greenhouse gases, with the objective of stabilizing their concentration. The difficulties in securing the effective implementation of this Accord are well known. But the challenge of limiting the extent of future global climate change is even greater. Implementation of the Kyoto Accord, in itself, is not likely to make a significant difference in the global climate situation, at least for a century. Economic growth among the emerging market and poorest countries will need to be fostered in an environmentally sustainable way if greenhouse gas stabilization is to occur. Moreover, industrial and developing countries face the difficult challenge of *adapting* to the climate change which *is* inevitably going to occur in coming decades.

In both developed and developing countries, fiscal policy will play an important role in facilitating a sustainable use of natural resources and in safeguarding the environment. For example, harmful subsidies and inappropriate tax policies that lead to the excessive exploitation of natural resources will need to be phased out. The prices of energy products will have to reflect their social costs. Subsidies for pesticides and fertilizer use – which contribute to over-farming of land – will need to be eliminated and replaced with government expenditure programmes that more directly benefit small farmers. At the same time, industrial countries must implement similar policies to ensure that the world's environmental resources are not overexploited.[5]

The IMF has emphasized the importance of considering whether or not the policies in Fund-supported programmes may have adverse environmental effects or whether there are environmental issues that are sufficiently important that they might influence the design of Fund programmes. Issues of environmental sustainability are also increasingly recognized, including with respect to taking account of environmental effects in more accurately measuring real growth rates.

Finally, in coming decades, other issues will confront the rich countries that will further complicate the global challenges faced by rich and poor countries alike. In particular, aging populations will add further fiscal pressures that will make it more difficult for the industrial countries to shoulder environmental sustainability programmes and additional foreign assistance to poor countries.

NOTES

1   *The Poverty Reduction and Growth Facility (PRGF) – Operational Issues* (Washington: International Monetary Fund, 13 December 13 1999).

2   Horst Köhler, *The Monterrey Consensus and Beyond: Moving from Vision to Action*, introductory remarks at the International Conference on Financing for Development, Monterrey, 21 March 2002.

3   Michel Camdessus, speech on *Development and Poverty Reduction: A Multilateral Approach* (Bangkok: International Monetary Fund, 2000).

4   Horst Köhler, *World Religions – Universal Peace – Global Ethics* (Washington, DC: International Monetary Fund, 19 September 2002).

5   International Monetary Fund, *Contribution to World Summit on Sustainable Development* (August/September 2002).

7

Commodification of Public Goods: Critique and Alternatives[1]

Patrick Bond

> Everyone has the right to an environment that is not harmful to their health or well-being... everyone has the right to have access to... sufficient water.[2]
>
> Bill of Rights, Constitution of the Republic of South Africa, 1996

The World Bank's Water Commodification Agenda

Are there intractable contradictions between a rights-based agenda, respectful of the social, ecological and spiritual characteristics of water, and an approach that emphasizes water as an economic good, a commodity? This essay demonstrates, in one of the most politicized and unequal environments in the world, that the contradictions can be debilitating and literally fatal.

The case study setting is important. In 2003, South Africa was an eco-social mess. The official government statistical agency released a report in October 2002 confirming that in real terms, average African household income had declined 19 per cent from 1995-2000, while white household income was up 15 per cent. The average black household earned a sixth as much as the average white household in 2000, down from a quarter in 1995. Households with less than R670 in monthly income – mainly black Africa, coloured and of Asian descent – increased from 20 per cent of the population in 1995 to 28 per cent in 2000. Across the racial divides, the poorest half of all South Africans earn just 9.7 per cent of national income, down from 11.4 per cent in 1995. The richest 20 per cent earn 65 per cent of all income. The official measure of unemployment rose from 15 per cent in 1995 to 30 per cent in 2000, and adding to that figure frustrated job-seekers brings the percentage of unemployed people to 43 per cent. These statistics reveal worsening poverty; one symptom is that 10 million people reported having had their water cut off in one national government survey, and 10 million were also victims of electricity disconnections, mainly due to unaffordability. In addition, 2 million people have been evicted from their homes or land since liberation in 1994.[3] Most other countries in Southern Africa show similar if not higher levels of poverty, unemployment and inequality.

There are several reasons why South/Southern Africa provides revealing material as a case study. In the mid-1990s the region began experiencing severe water stresses (e.g. the drought of 1995, and persistent problems of municipal payment arrears by low-income residents across Southern Africa). The World Bank began issuing documents and making presentations in South Africa not only about macro-economic strategy, where the Bank contributed its econometric models and staff to pursue the failed 'Growth, Employment and Redistribution' strategy, as well as similar policies in other countries. In addition, the Bank advised Pretoria politicians and bureaucrats about efficient water management, ranging from pricing of water to infrastructure investment to natural resources management. Finally, the Bank has adopted South African lessons in its *World Development Report 2004: Making Services Work for Poor People*, in so far as 'Chapter 10: Water and Sanitation' intends using case studies of local government boundaries; 'greater separation of roles between policy makers and service providers'; 'designing pricing and subsidy strategies to ensure both accountability and protection of poor people'; 'capturing the political economy window of restructuring local governments'; 'addressing the cost of transitions – the role of public finance from central governments'; and 'delivering and supporting the capacity of local governments during the process of decentralization'.[4]

Some Bank statements, such as the book *African Water Resources*, are vague and all encompassing: 'The strategy developed in this document is based on the principle that water is a scarce good with dimensions of economic efficiency, social equity, and environmental sustainability'.[5] However, others – including one termed 'instrumental' in the World Bank's 1999 *South Africa Country Assistance Strategy* – played a crucial role in the disconnection of water supplies to millions of low-income South Africans, in the ongoing outbreak of cholera, in the highly controversial privatization of municipal water, and in the reorientation of national water priorities towards a market-based system.

This essay documents some of the specific and general problems associated with a dogmatic 'neoliberal' approach to water that, during the late 1990s, became official policy at the Bretton Woods institutions (the World Bank and International Monetary Fund), notwithstanding the numerous dangers and well-tested alternative approaches (recognized inside the Bank from time to time). South Africa and the surrounding semi-arid region of Southern Africa represent good terrain upon which to observe World Bank water management strategies. The region has specific problems not only with natural cycles of droughts and floods, which have been exacerbated by global warming. In addition, the skewed settler-colonial mining and agricultural systems and economic development patterns make future conflict over water a certainty. Water has already served as an important lubricant of sustained geopolitical strife in Lesotho (1998) and on the Namibia/Botswana border (ongoing). Problems also arose in relation to flood control on South African sourced rivers that flow into Mozambique during 2000-1. Historically, the conflict over water was the source of sustained colonial and apartheid oppression: for example, large dams displaced tens of thousands of people on the Zambezi River (Kariba and Cahorra Bassa dams) and Orange River (Garieb Dam).

For our purposes, it may be most important to highlight the micro-economics of water pricing and public utility management, for it is here that contrasts between water as a commodity and water as a social/spiritual/ecological good are greatest. Specifically, this essay objects to the user-pay full-cost-recovery approach that is most strongly and universally promoted by the World Bank across Africa. So it is to both the Bank's urban water utility reforms and rural project principles that we turn first for general evidence of the contradictions that inevitably emerge, prior to investigating the Bank's role in South and Southern African water privatization debates.

Water, Power and Poverty
Recovery from a major conflict, whether civil or liberation in nature, ideally entails large investments in water infrastructure, in part so as to bring about the return of displaced rural people to their traditional homes. Donors have often played a central role in providing water to impoverished people whose own resources would not sustain either capital investments or recurrent costs (operating and maintenance costs of water services ranging from bulk supply to household reticulation and smallholder irrigation). The importance of managing water extends up from micro-project level to national, regional and international policy, and donor agencies have played crucial roles at all levels.

The Bretton Woods institutions' central coordinating and strategizing role in South and Southern Africa water management deserves detailed consideration. The International Monetary Fund has drawn many water-related issues into its own structural adjustment programmes, whether the Enhanced Structural Adjustment Facility, Poverty Reduction and Growth Facility or Poverty Reduction Strategy Programme.[6] According to one recent report,

> A review of IMF loan policies in 40 random countries reveals that, during 2000, IMF loan agreements in 12 countries included conditions imposing water privatization or full cost recovery. In general, it is African countries, and the smallest, poorest and most debt-ridden countries, that are being subjected to IMF conditions on water privatization and full cost recovery.[7]

However, it is the IMF's fraternal organization, the World Bank, that has had primary responsibilities for intellectual, policy and project promotion consistent with water commodification, so the Bank is the main focus of our immediate interests. Moreover, by the late 1990s, the Bank had become involved in a wide variety of Southern African water-related projects with other donors.[8] The Bank maintains a broadly dominant role in proffering advice – and sometimes giving orders – in the regional water sector.[9] Internationally, the Bank website lists the following key international relationships – several of which were catalysed by the Bank – in advancing its water agenda:
• Global Water Partnership, which has the mandate of developing networks and knowledge for water resources management, and is based in Stockholm.
• World Commission on Dams, which was launched by IUCN/World Conservation Union and the World Bank, together with many other partners, which is defining standards for when, where and how dams should be designed, constructed and operated.
• Water and Sanitation Programme, a 20-year-old partnership hosted by the Bank to improve access of poor people to water and sanitation services.

- Business Partnership for Development, hosted by the NGO Wateraid in London, to develop innovative mechanisms for ensuring that private water contracts serve the needs of the poor.
- International Programme for Technological Research in Irrigation and Drainage, hosted by the Food and Agricultural Organization in Rome, which has the objective of developing innovative technologies for irrigation and drainage.

The Bank is a regular coordinator of, and leverage point for, donor resources. It is a catalyst for several large dam projects, a project and water sector lender, a 'Knowledge Bank' source of information, a facilitator of civil-society involvement and promoter of a limited version of 'community participation' in water projects. The Bank is also a government policy adviser, an investor in privatized water infrastructure (through the International Finance Corporation), a host to numerous African water agencies' Water Utilities Partnership, and the main agency imposing stipulations upon water sector management via structural adjustment and debt relief conditionality. The Bank can, therefore, claim not only to have a coherent perspective and wide-ranging market-oriented framework, but also to have applied these to water projects and policy across Africa. The African Development Bank has generally followed the same patterns.[10]

True, there are occasional disagreements among Bank staff. A mid-1990s debate occurred over whether retail water prices should follow a rising block tariff or instead more closely approximate the cost of production ('full cost recovery'). The victory of the latter argument within the Bank during the late 1990s seemed to herald an era of full-fledged water commodification, while at the same time the Bretton Woods institutions were most dogmatically insistent upon similar principles in relation to macro-economic policy: in a phrase, 'get the prices right'.

The philosophical underpinning to this dogmatic approach was once expressed in an infamous memo by the Bank's then chief economist, Lawrence Summers. 'I think the economic logic behind dumping a load of toxic waste in the lowest-wage country is impeccable and we should face up to that', Summers argued in a 1991 memo that was subsequently leaked and published in *The Economist*.[11] Rather than 'internalize the externalities' associated with pollution or ecological damage, the ready solution is simply to displace these to somewhere where political power is negligible and the immediate environmental implications are less visible, in the name of overall economic growth. After all, Summers continued, inhabitants of low-income countries typically die before the age at which they would begin suffering prostate cancer associated with toxic dumping. And in any event, using 'marginal productivity' as a measure, low-income Africans are not worth very much anyhow. Nor are Africans' aesthetic concerns with air pollution likely to be as substantive as they are for wealthy northerners. Although Summers and his colleague Lant Pritchett have retrospectively used the term 'ironic' to describe the argument, *The Economist* endorsed the underlying principle by which ecological and social objectives are subordinated to 'impeccable' economic logic. Indeed, it can be argued that the subsequent decade of Washington Consensus commandments – 'getting the prices right' – no matter the social costs, codified the Bretton Woods approach.[12]

But just as important as the ideology of commodification are the numerous practical applications. Bank experience is drawn upon from across the world. In conjunction with the UNDP, the Bank-catalysed World Water Forum – a crucial session of which was held in Kyoto in March 2003 – has become the leading international forum for applying market solutions to water-related problems. The Bank also sponsored the World Commission on Dams, which included studies and submissions concerning two Southern African megadams: Kariba and Garieb. The region's two largest dams, Kariba (late 1950s) and the Lesotho Highlands Water Project (1980s-present), were both catalysed and funded by the Bank.

Also of critical importance is the role of Bank water management in grassroots-level conflict resolution – via development projects such as water supply enhancement that can resolve longstanding disputes, or via restructuring riparian water law so as to end centralized administrative allocation of water, to be replaced by water trading in specially designed markets. In virtually all such cases, the Bank has developed policies and projects that further the commodification of water.

Commodifying water entails the following:
- highlighting its role mainly as an 'economic good';
- attempting to reduce cross-subsidization that distorts the end-user price of water (tariff);
- insisting upon 100 per cent cost recovery on operating and maintenance costs (even if capital investments are subsidized);
- promoting a severely limited form of means-tested subsidization;
- establishing shadow prices for water as an environmental good;
- solving problems associated with state control of water (inefficiencies, excessive administrative centralization, lack of competition, unaccounted-for-water, weak billing and political interference), and in the process;
- fostering the conditions for water privatization.

Concrete manifestations are obvious once we consider two recent Africa-wide Bank statements on water resources management, urban and rural, that provide the conceptual underpinning for water projects and policies. We can then consider other evidence of the role of the Bretton Woods institutions in promoting privatization of water in Southern Africa.

Urban Utility Reform

The Kampala Statement of February 2001, drafted by the Bank in association with the Water Utilities Partnership, is an important review and aspirational vision of broader water policy issues in Africa, in part because of buy-in from African water officials.[13] The Kampala Statement is a misleading document, for it certainly makes a strong case that poor people, and women in particular, deserve primary consideration in water policy. However, the actual content of the statement – and all the follow-up work planned – is very much towards market-oriented reforms and what can be termed 'privatization', a word that encompasses various types of management, outsourcing and ownership relations by which for-profit firms come to operate what were once state water services. A typical premise is the notion that 'the poor are willing and have the capacity to pay for services that are adapted to their needs'. And dealing with the semantics of privatization, the Kampala Statement suggests:

> Reforms should not be considered synonymous with privatization, but as a coordinated series of structural changes to provide better water and sanitation services to more and more people. However, an increased role of the private sector in WSS delivery has been a dominant feature of the reform processes of African countries as it has been recognized as a viable alternative to public service delivery and financial autonomy.

Indeed, the premise of water privatization had already been cemented. Not surprisingly, omitted from the Kampala Statement is any substantive information that would assist African policy makers understand and address – even via 'regulation' – four crucial drawbacks to such private partnerships:

1. The high profit-rate extractions, in hard currency, typically demanded by transnational corporations.[14]
2. The issue of whether hard-currency Bank loans are required to promote water privatization.[15]
3. The change in the incentive structure of water supply once private suppliers begin operating (especially in relation to pricing).[16]
4. The difficulty of a private supplier recognizing and internalizing positive socio-environmental externalities.[17]

Aside from private sector involvement, another feature of the Kampala Statement is the strong orientation towards water-system cost recovery. As a result, the statement denies the most fundamental reality faced by water services providers:

> The objectives of addressing the needs of the poor and ensuring cost recovery for utility companies are not in contradiction; well thought-out mechanisms for cross-subsidies, alternative service provision, and easing the cash flow demands upon the poor can allow the utility to survive whilst attending to their needs.

There is an enormous contradiction, in reality, between the drive to cost recovery and the needs of the poor (as well as other vulnerable groups, and the environment), as discussed below. In particular, as we will see, the pressure to corporatize/privatize water services works decisively against cross-subsidization.

The incentive to reform in a neoliberal mode is the universally acknowledged fact that African water systems don't work well, especially when associated with public utilities that enjoy a relaxed budget constraint (i.e. ongoing subsidies from general revenues). Progressive critics of the African state, dating at least as far back as Frantz Fanon in *The Wretched of the Earth*, typically point to a variety of features of neo-colonialism, compradorism, neoliberal economic pressures, petit-bourgeois bureaucratic class formation, and simple power relations whereby elites can garner far more resources from local states than can the masses.

In contrast, the Kampala Statement derives the problems from one fundamental cause, namely, Africans get the prices 'wrong': 'The poor performance of a number of public utilities is rooted in a policy of repressed tariffs which leads to lack of investment, poor maintenance lagging coverage, and subsidized services reserved for the privileged who are connected to the network'. The mandate for full cost recovery and an end to cross-subsidies – with meagre subsidies allegedly to be available for poor people at some future date – follows logically. As a result, one of the most important issues associated with water resource management – abuse of water by large-scale agro-corporate irrigation and wealthy consumers – is barely remarked upon, and the word 'conservation' is only used once, in passing.

Politically, the Kampala Statement is extremely naive – or disingenuous: 'Labour can also be a powerful ally in explaining the benefits of the reform to the general public. It is essential therefore that the utility workers themselves understand and appreciate the need for the reform.' But as shown in the conclusion to this essay, political resistance is probably the most interesting contradiction embedded within the Bank's water strategy.

Water for Rural Villages

Moving to the countryside, the Bank strategy is also articulated in the *Sourcebook on Community Driven Development in the Africa Region – Community Action Programs*.[18] According to the sourcebook, the Bank has played a key role in moving African water projects out of their previous unsustainable, failure-riven mode:

> Twenty-five years ago handpumps designed for North American farmsteads were installed in villages across Africa. They all broke down shortly after being installed. Twenty years ago robust handpumps and centralized maintenance was introduced. All the pumps broke down within one year and took months to repair. Donors were spending more and more money to maintain what was installed and less and less on new facilities.
>
> Fifteen years ago, community-based management and user-friendly handpumps were introduced, together with VIP latrines. Communities had to manage and pay for the maintenance of their handpumps. The approach was received with great scepticism by sector ministries: 'Villagers can't possibly maintain a pump'. Today, community-based management is accepted by all sector professionals across Africa as the only sustainable approach to village water supply and sanitation (with construction of low-cost latrines) and increasingly to town water supply. Demand responsiveness where communities choose the facilities they want, decide how to manage and finance them, and pay part of the capital cost is also widely accepted as fundamental to sustainability.[19]

Yet the neoliberal, state-shrinking project-level work is not yet complete until the central philosophy associated with neoliberal water policy is adopted. According to the *Sourcebook*:

> Promote increased capital cost recovery from users. An upfront cash contribution based on their willingness-to-pay is required from users to demonstrate demand and develop community capacity to administer funds and tariffs. Ensure 100 per cent recovery of operation and maintenance costs.[20]

The Bank's Role in South African Water Commodification

The 100 per cent cost-recovery philosophy became extremely controversial in Africa's most industrialized country, South Africa. Before providing details, it is useful to consider at least one reflection of the relations between the Bank and Pretoria. A major report by the International Center for Investigative Journalism in February 2003 explored the issue:[21]

> According to a 1999 World Bank strategy report, the bank played an important role in charting South Africa's privatization strategy. It used South Africa as a sort of test laboratory to 'pilot our evolving role as a "knowledge bank"', the report stated.
>
> 'The Bank has provided technical assistance and policy advice in virtually all sectors of the economy', Pamela Cox, World Bank director for South Africa, wrote in the introduction to *South Africa Country Assistance Strategy*, a Bank report. The report stated that the Bank's International Financial Corporation has played an 'active role in the further development of infrastructure in South Africa and promoted the increased participation of the private sector in this area'.

The same 1999 document concluded with a proud claim: advice by 'knowledge bank' water expert John Roome in October 1995 was 'instrumental in facilitating a radical revision in South Africa's approach to bulk water management'.[22] Although the presentation dealt with the transition from national-scale (bulk) 'riparian rights' to a water-market strategy ultimately adopted in a 1998 policy and law, the micro-economics of water pricing were also crucial.

The debate at the time was whether a 1994 Reconstruction and Development Programme (RDP) medium-term mandate for free 'lifeline' water supplies of 50-60 litres of water per person per day in urban areas would be provided, or whether instead water should not be subsidized (aside from capital investments) but rather priced according to marginal cost. Roome argued municipal water privatization contracts 'would be much harder to establish' if poor consumers had the expectation of getting something for nothing, i.e. the lifeline supply mandated in the RDP. Moreover, if consumers didn't pay their water bills, Roome continued, South African water minister Kader Asmal needed a 'credible threat of cutting service'.[23] In short, a private supplier logically objects to serving low-income people with even a small lifeline consumption amount. Hence the demand for such a rising block tariff is indeed, as Roome pointed out, a serious deterrent to privatization. The most important point about the advice on micro-economic pricing is how it led to distributionally regressive outcomes in South Africa's cities, and caused a cholera epidemic in the rural areas.

Pricing Towards Marginal Cost

Probably the two most important reflections of the dangers of marginal cost pricing – i.e. 'getting the prices right' by following 'impeccable economic logic' so as to attract private sector investors into the water sector – are ecologically disastrous supply enhancements in the form of mega-dams that allow for increased hedonistic consumption on the one hand; and on the other hand, price increases plus water disconnection policies which kill low-income people who cannot afford their water bills, through cholera, diarrhoea and other water-borne diseases (many of which lead to HIV-Aids opportunistic infections).

In the first category, an extreme but emblematic case is the Lesotho Highlands Water Project (LHWP). To prevent construction of further large dams for the purpose of cross-catchment water transfer from the Lesotho mountains to Johannesburg, residents of Alexandra township filed a World Bank Inspection Panel complaint about the Bank's failure to consider 'demand-side management' as an alternative. Central to the latter strategy is penalizing hedonistic water consumers through higher tariffs. The Bank's Inspection Panel inexplicably turned down the township activists' request to simply carry out a formal investigation into the distributional problem.

Alexandra residents complained to the Bank Inspection Panel: 'The possibility for changing water usage patterns through progressive block tariffs was never factored in to LHWP demand calculations, in part because key World Bank staff (though not the Bank's Washington headquarters) explicitly opposed differential pricing of water'.[24] The residents referred to Roome's October 1995 presentation to Asmal, which argued against sliding tariffs, citing in particular the case of Johannesburg.

At the time, Johannesburg (known then as the 'Central Wits' region) had a four-block tariff structure which rose gradually from R1.20/Kl for 0-10 Kls per month, up to R3/Kl for more than 45 Kl/month consumption. Roome's only valid criticism of Johannesburg's water pricing model was that the rising block tariffs 'may limit options with respect to tertiary providers – in particular private concessions much harder to establish'.[25]

This criticism is understandable, although not forgivable, in view of the World Bank goal to privatize municipal water. Private bidders would indeed be deterred if they encountered an obligation to consider redistribution – in the form of a lifeline water supply and a sharply rising tariff for hedonistic users – when pricing water to maximize profit. The reason for this is that the firm's curves for marginal cost (each additional unit) and marginal revenue (ideally running parallel, so as to 'get the prices right') necessarily depart from a redistributive water pricing structure.

Most South African cities moved in Roome's favoured direction, i.e. away from cross-subsidization, prior to the ANC's September 2000 promise of a free lifeline water supply and rising block tariff. Tellingly, instead of raising the slope of Johannesburg's near-flat block tariff to levels that would have achieved social justice and conservation, the city managers hired World Bank consultants as part of the Igoli 2002 corporatization programme. The city's strategy, until July 2001, was to provide only a small grant – R30 per month for water and a bit more for other services – to 'indigent' households whose poverty status could be confirmed through stigma-inducing 'means-testing'. Instead of finding several hundred thousand qualified households, the city signed up only a meagre 24,000 recipients.[26]

Across Gauteng, prior to the implementation of the free water policy, the Palmer Development Group found in its survey of Rand Water Board users that low-volume users had systematically been charged more than higher-volume users since 1996:

> It is evident that there is a continuing increase in tariffs in real terms, of the order of 7 per cent per year for all blocks. Some of this increase may be related to increasing bulk supply costs and some may relate to improved service. But there is a concern that a part of the increase relates to decreasing efficiency. A further concern is that the lowest block is the one which is increasing fastest.[27]

Indeed, among the municipalities served by Rand Water during the late 1990s, those at the first block of consumption paid 39 per cent more, *after inflation*, than they had in 1996. The more hedonistic consumers' rate went up only 24 per cent, as shown in the table.

Table 1: Residential water tariff increases imposed by Rand Water-supplied municipalities, 1996-2000 (rands per thousand litres, real 2000 currency).[28]

Tariff	1996	1997	1998	1999	2000	96-00 % rise
Block 1	1.86	1.97	2.33	2.41	2.58	39 per cent
Block 2	2.52	2.64	3.26	3.22	3.36	33 per cent
Block 3	2.91	3.01	3.66	3.71	3.79	30 per cent
Block 4	3.49	3.41	4.20	4.20	4.32	24 per cent

The reverse Robin Hood policy ended finally, after July 2001, when the free services policy was partially adopted in Gauteng cities. At that point, Johannesburg adjusted its tariff curve in a slightly more progressive direction. Beyond the free 6 kl/household/month, a R2.30/kl price was applied up to 10 kl/h/m. From 10-15 kl/h/m, the tariff was for R4.10/kl; from 15-20 kl/h/m, R4.60; from 25-40 kl/h/m, R5.50/kl; and above 40 kl/h/m, R6.50.29.[29]

What would that mean, price-wise, for a grandmother in a township looking after a dozen dependents on a measly monthly pension? Even after July 2000 when the new free water policy allegedly came into effect, if she and the others consumed the 50 litres recommended for human health and hygiene each day, the roughly 20 kl per month would cost R53 in Johannesburg, nearly a tenth of her monthly income. In some towns served by Rand

Water, the cost would be yet higher: R90 in Randfontein, and more than R75 in Emfuleni, Lesedi, Midvaal and Highveld East.

As for industrial tariffs, they have been kept on a regressive schedule, so that extremely high-volume users (in excess of a million litres per month) pay declining rates in many towns supplied by Rand Water. In Johannesburg the tariff was set at R4.60 in July 2001.

What this suggests is that in South Africa's cities, the commercialization and privatization process favoured by the World Bank and IMF has had regressive impacts, *even after* a promise of 6,000 litres per household per month was made by the ruling party. But things are even worse in rural South Africa.

Project Failure

After a 1994 White Paper was adopted by water minister Asmal, very much in the spirit of the World Bank's *Sourcebook on Community Driven Development* (in so far as prohibiting subsidies on operating and maintenance costs), the Department of Water Affairs and Forestry (Dwaf) began their famous capital investment roll-out. Dwaf officials instructed staff and all agencies carrying out community water supply and sanitation activities on its behalf to implement the White Paper standards and tariffs to the letter. Community water supply projects include communal standpipes at 200-metre intervals. Despite the array of problems associated with collecting payment for water from communal standpipes, the principle of full payment for the operating, maintenance and replacement costs was insisted upon. Once projects were built, especially by Mvula Trust and other non-governmental suppliers, communities didn't receive further support.

Inexorably, extremely serious problems arose in the community water supply projects. There are varying estimates about project sustainability, with even the pro-government Mvula Trust acknowledging that roughly half of the projects it established would fail because of inability to maintain the system. The official Dwaf line by the early 2000s was that more than 80 per cent of the taps were still working, but there were *no* national monitoring and evaluation reviews, merely tortured extrapolations of dubious small-scale reviews. One oral report by Dwaf official Helgard Muller in 1999 put the government's own cost recovery on these projects at just 1 per cent.

Reasons for unsustainability invariably include very real affordability constraints and an unwillingness to pay for communal standpipes. Communal standpipes are often not viewed as a significant improvement on existing sources of water. Other important reasons for failure include poor quality of construction, areas within communities without service and intermittent supply.

Moreover, the community water supply systems have led to numerous instances of inequity. Adjacent communities pay different amounts depending on the systems installed. Rural households pay for water from standpipes, whereas households in Durban obtaining water on site were getting the first 6 kilolitres per month for free, i.e. the amount of the break-even point between the cost of collecting payment and the amount collected. Communities with new water systems were paying for the ongoing functioning of their systems, whereas communities supplied by the former Bantustan governments often received their water for free. Such inequities led to significant levels of community tension within and between villages. And, despite the claim to provide 'some to all', vast areas did not receive water services of any sort.

Dwaf's response to the high level of subsequent project failure was initially to move yet further from the entitlement to water as spelt out in the Constitution, partly egged on by advisers from international agencies such as the World Bank.[30] Dwaf continued to insist upon construction of communal standpipes in rural areas, but in future they were to be built with prepaid meters, whereby people must buy electronic cards to access even communally piped water, a system declared illegal in Britain.[31]

Instead of moving towards the medium-term aim of the RDP and providing taps on site, the department proved willing to relax the 200-metre criterion and allow for standpipes further apart so as to limit the number and thereby cost of prepaid meters. Indeed, one Dwaf document circulating widely in early 1999 recommended that water supply to rural people be dropped from 25 to 7 litres per person per day.[32] One of the central problems, Dwaf officials continued to insist, was financing the expansion of water supplies to low-income people. As the free-services promise was unpacked, Dwaf director general Mike Muller issued several statements confirming that no additional national subsidy funds were available to make good on the water promise.[33] To the suggestion that Dwaf tax the abuse of water by commercial agriculture and, as a short-term measure, use defence force tanker supplies to those with no access, Muller responded that 'no case for new money can be made until it is clear that existing funds are being properly used'.[34]

Yet because of the neoliberal policy parameters, the existing funding for rural projects was not being properly used. Failure to spend Dwaf's budget had been an embarrassment dating to the mid-1990s, when the majority of water project funds were rolled over, back to the finance ministry. Yet Dwaf's 100 per cent cost-recovery strategy was based upon the alleged lack of sufficient funding, and the government continued avoiding the option of taxing large-volume water consumers.

Water Denialism
Demands to reverse the government's full cost-recovery policy by labour and social movements were made during the late 1990s, and Asmal's mid-1999 replacement, Kasrils, began hinting at a policy change in February 2000 after rural water projects broke down at a dramatic rate – mainly because impoverished residents could not keep the vital service maintained by themselves without a subsidy, as Asmal had demanded. When cholera broke out in August 2000, less than four months before nationwide municipal elections, the ANC government reacted by promising a free services lifeline. It was progress, although for poor households the promise was half the amount needed, and for electricity was undefined, but in practice amounted to only a tenth of essential needs.

As might have been predicted, the World Bank saw Kasrils' and the ANC's free-services promise as potentially dangerous. In March 2000 the Bank's Orwellian *Sourcebook on Community Driven Development in the Africa Region* laid out the policy on pricing water: 'Work is still needed with political leaders in some national governments to move away from the concept of free water for all'.[35]

Social disasters from such rigid neoliberal policy were strewn across Africa, especially when low-income people simply could not afford any state services, or cut back on girls' schooling or healthcare when cost recovery became burdensome. In October 2000 the Bank was instructed by the US Congress never to impose these user-fee provisions on education and healthcare, and in 2002 a campaign by progressive NGOs in the US expanded to decommodify water as well.

As one example, in 1996 the World Bank and IMF launched its 'Highly-Indebted Poor Countries' (HIPC) initiative, and Mozambique was a high-profile pilot project. But harsh conditions were set to the paltry debt relief, as expressed in a letter sent to Mozambican president Joaqim Chissano by World Bank president James Wolfensohn in March 1998:

- the privatization of municipal water (which required, in classical public-squeeze prior to private profiteering, the 'sharp' rise in water tariffs, which were 'to be increased even further prior to the signing of management contracts');
- the quintupling of patient fees for public health services over a five-year period;
- the privatization and simultaneous liberalization of the important cashew nut processing industry (which led to the collapse of most factories and 10,000 job losses, mainly women).[36]

A year later, more than seventy new conditions emerged in the next IMF debt relief package, including a recommendation that parliament make the tax structure more regressive (i.e. so the rich would pay a decreasing share of their income). Yet more arrogantly, the IMF used new jargon in applying neoliberal conditionality to the rural water sector: 'transforming the planning and delivery of rural water and sanitation services from a supply-driven model to a sustained demand responsive model, characterized by community management, cost recovery, and the involvement of the private sector'.[37] Such a 'demand-responsive approach' is an increasingly discredited development strategy. Such cost-recovery strategies simply don't work in a country in which 70 per cent of the population live below the poverty line.

In 1999, however, increased public pressure against the IMF and Bank – including Chissano's own public frustration over HIPC – led to slightly greater concessions for Mozambique (repayments fell to $73 million and then $58 million by 2001). Nevertheless, the IMF and Bank remained so callous to Mozambique's grinding poverty, and were unmoved even by the January-February 2000 floods that devastated Mozambique. Instead of shaking loose more debt cancellation, Washington offered only to reschedule repayment, by adding the amount due that year to the end of the amortization schedule.

Thus for one of the world's poorest countries, the experience of HIPC debt relief shows how the combination of international financial power, unrepayable debt and the Washington Consensus economic philosophy can be a lethal combination, via water privatization.

A final example of the denial of water/sanitation through the privatization process is found in the continent's wealthiest city, Johannesburg. The World Bank played a substantial role in designing Igoli 2002, the plan to corporatize Johannesburg utilities. The Johannesburg Water Company, also managed by Suez, soon controversially introduced pit latrines in spite of porous soil and the spread of the *E.coli* bacteria, so as to prevent poor people flushing their toilets with water that they would not be able to afford given Johannesburg Water's pricing strategy. The company also offers a low-flush 'shallow sewage' system to residents of 'condominium' (single-storey) houses arranged in rows, connected to each other by sanitation pipes much closer to the surface. Given the limited role of gravity in the gradient and the mere trickle of water that flows through, community residents are required to negotiate with each other over who will physically unblock sewers every three months. Prepaid water metres – outlawed in Britain – are also associated with Johannesburg Water's attempt to limit consumption by the poorest urban residents.

Conclusion: Resisting the BWIs and Claiming the Right to Water
It should be evident by now that the World Bank and IMF have been violating the rights to water that are explicitly guaranteed by the South African Constitution and implicitly crucial to any humane development strategy for the people of Southern Africa, and the world. They have done so by ignoring several aspects of water, discussed above.

The Bank and IMF ignore 'positive externalities' of publicly provided water:
- public health improvements achieved through water-borne disease mitigation;
- gender equity, through permanent access by women to water;
- environmental protection, through protection of local ecosystems instead of their degradation as water collection points and run-offs for informal sewage/sanitation;
- economic multipliers that stem from access to water;
- desegregation that can be achieved through standardized, higher-quality water/sanitation services.

It should be evident from this list of 'public goods' and 'merit goods' that *only the state and society* have a material incentive in these sorts of positive externalities, and that private, for-profit suppliers do not (except in extremely rare cases when they run local clinics as well).

In addition, since water infrastructure is a classical natural monopoly, and since investments in the sector tend to be 'lumpy', there is a sustained reason for public, not private, provision of water services.

As for those advocating both privatization and regulation, the difficulty of the latter is evident in most cases, given the weakness of states, and the long history of water-sector corruption by multinational corporations.

Finally, the crises in the state water sector, and the lack of capital that states have to invest – the two main reasons for advocating privatization – are in fact due mainly to the failed 1980s-1990s structural adjustment programmes, to corrupt state bureaucrats, to weak trade unions and to disempowered consumers/communities. These are all temporary problems which can be overcome through a concerted political effort and a redirection of state resources that are currently being used for debt repayments – to the same World Bank and IMF which push privatization because states lack money and capacity.

Across the world, people have begun to unite in defence of their human right to water, in part on spiritual grounds but also out of pure necessity. Whether in Cochabamba, Bolivia, or Accra, Ghana, or Atlanta, Georgia, or Buenos Aires, Argentina, or Manila in the Philippines, or Johannesburg, the ongoing anti-privatization campaigns for water access are resonating with struggles in other places to *decommodify* water and institute public sector services that meet people's needs. Whether through public-public partnerships, public-people arrangements between states and communities, or public-proletarian partnerships involving the municipal workers' unions, the advantages of social determination of water systems are far greater than the fleeting efficiency gains that may, in the short term, arise from public-private partnerships.

A statement by the Ralph Nader-linked organization Public Citizen lists ten reasons to oppose water privatization:
- privatization leads to rate increases;
- privatization undermines water quality;
- companies are accountable to shareholders not consumers;
- privatization fosters corruption;
- privatization reduces local control and public rights;
- private financing costs more than public financing;
- privatization leads to job losses;
- privatization is difficult to reverse;
- privatization can leave the poor with no access to clean water;
- privatization would open the door for bulk water exports.[38]

Several of these propositions are already manifestly obvious in South Africa. The Southern African experience suggests that even if in South Africa there is strong resistance to privatization, the rest of the region remains under threat. And in South Africa it took a great deal of time and social discontent to roll back the tide of privatization, even after the late 1990s witnessed extensive technical arguments about the merits of public, not private, provision of water.

What these debates suggest is that the World Bank – as one of the most important development agencies, and a source of immense power during periods of fiscal stress – is not learning these lessons. Many of its documents released since the beginning of the millennium continue to force-feed the discredited Washington Consensus approach. Lawrence Summers' 'impeccable economic logic' – fatal if the advice is followed – has its successor in World Bank and IMF strategies to remove water from the public sphere, and reduce it to a mere commodity.

What kinds of resistance is the world beginning to witness? There are several international lobbies to force WB/IMF/WTO to stop commodifying water and other services. In South Africa in particular, a campaign by the SA Municipal Workers Union and the Rural Development Services Network for free lifeline water (50 litres per person per day) continues – as do numerous community struggles against water commodification and privatization. Indeed, Anti-Privatization Forums and other manifestations of the Global Justice Movement exist in many Southern African cities: Johannesburg, Cape Town, Durban, Pholokwane, Harare, Bulawayo, Mbabane, Lilongwe and Windhoek. A Southern African People's Solidarity Network links progressive activists, churches, trade unions and think-tanks, as does a regional water-sector network.

More generally, to resist World Bank and IMF power, Jubilee movements across the region continue fighting for debt repudiation. The African Social Forum is developing tough positions. And most Southern African progressive movements are demanding that the IMF and World Bank should immediately quit their countries. To drive home the point in a manner which image-conscious international financiers understand, lawsuits are being filed against those banks (including, soon, the World Bank and IMF) which supported apartheid and dictatorships.

The financial squeeze is what the Bank and IMF have used to get their way. Likewise, a financial sanctions campaign against the Bank began in April 2000, called for by Jubilee South Africa, the Brazilian Movement of the Landless, and a Haitian social-justice coalition (PAPDA). They immediately asked the question posed, first and foremost, during South African apartheid: who reaps the economic benefits of systemic oppression? Today, churches, other socially responsible investors, trade unions, municipalities and universities together ponder a similar query: is it morally acceptable to earn profits from World Bank bonds (responsible for 80 per cent of World Bank funding) if the Bank so evidently contributes to what Thabo Mbeki terms 'global apartheid'?

Having answered in the negative, many people of conscience are joining the World Bank Bonds Boycott (WBBB), which sends a tough signal to the Bank: end anti-social, environmentally destructive activities and cancel Third World debt. When enough investors endorse the campaign, the Bank will suffer a declining bond rating, making it also *fiduciarily irresponsible* to invest, which in turn will represent a profound threat, a 'run on the Bank'. Recognizing the merits of the WBBB for changing power relations between the Bank and its many victims, dozens of major investors have endorsed the boycott, including church and religious community investors: the Unitarian Universalist General Assembly, the Conference of Major Superiors of Men, Pax Christi, USA and various denominations of Marianists, Sisters of the Holy

Cross, Franciscan Friars, Adrian Dominicans and many others. Adding their own muscle are ethical investment funds that include major players such as the Calvert Group, Trillium Assets Management, Progressive Assets Management, the Pax World Fund Family, Ben and Jerry's Foundation, the Global Greengrants Fund and the Citizens Funds. Finally, the WBBB has also undergone extensive discussions and debates in many US cities (e.g. San Francisco, Milwaukee, Oakland, Cambridge) and major trade union pension/investment funds (e.g. Teamsters, Postal Workers, Service Employees International, American Federation of Government Employees, Longshoremen, Communication Workers of America, and United Electrical, Radio and Machine Workers). In most cases, the decision by democratically elected decision makers to join the WBBB was unanimous.

It is likely that the denominations supportive of the World Council of Churches will also be asked by their memberships whether investing in global apartheid makes sense. There are many reasons to support the WBBB: the people who are intent on making water a human and spiritual good, not a for-profit commodity, have some of the strongest arguments to weaken Washington and save lives in the process.

NOTES

1   This material is partially based upon work previously published in P. Bond (2002), *Unsustainable South Africa: Environment, Development and Social Protest*, London, Merlin Press and Pietermaritzburg, University of Natal Press. Support for the analysis was provided by the University of Natal School of Development Studies research programme on donor roles in post-conflict societies, and by numerous colleagues who worked on these issues with me, especially through the Municipal Services Project (http://www.queensu.ca/msp).

2   Republic of South Africa (1996), *The Constitution of the Republic of South Africa*, Act 108 of 1996, Cape Town, s.24.a, s.27.1).

3   *Business Day*, 22 November 2002; Human Sciences Research Council and Municipal Services Project survey of disconnections analysed at http://www.queensu.ca/msp.

4   World Bank (2003), *Draft World Development Report 2004: Outline*, Washington, DC, http://www.worldbank.org, ch. 10, pp. 49-55.

5   World Bank (1996), *African Water Resources*, Technical Paper 331, Washington, DC, p. ix.

6   See, for example, http://www.challengeglobalization.org and S. Grusky, (2001), 'IMF makes Water Privatization Condition of Financial Support', PSIRU update, http://www.psiru.org.

7   R. Hennig (2001), 'IMF forces African Countries to Privatize Water', 8 February (http://www.afrol.com).

8   E. Soderstrom (1998), 'Survey of Donor Involvement in the Water Sector in the SADC Region', USAID, Gabarone, Botswana (cited on Africa Water Page).

9   In 2001 the Bank had numerous ongoing SADC water projects underway. In Angola, Bank projects include urban water supply and sanitation in the Luanda Water Supply project. The main Lesotho projects are the Highlands Water Project, Phase 1B and Water Sector Reform. The main Malawi project is National Water Development. Mauritius has a

Bank Environmental Sewerage and Sanitation project. Mozambique has a National Water I and National Water II. The Bank promoted the Aguas de Mocambique 15-year lease contract for Maputo and four identical five-year management contracts for four other cities. Companies benefiting include Saur International (France), IPE-Aguas de Portugal (Portugal) and Mazi-Mozambique (Mozambican). In Namibia the Bank is involved in bulk water commercialization through Namibia Water Corporation (NamWater). In South Africa private water contracts – pushed by the Bank originally in 1994 – include Johannesburg's Igoli 2002 and privatization in three other towns (Queenstown, Fort Beaufort and Stutterheim), as well as Dolphin Coast and Nelspruit. The main companies are Suez, Northumbrian, Saur, Biwater/Nuon and Vivendi. In Tanzania the Bank promoted privatization through the Dar es Salaam Water Supply and Sanitation Project, and a rural water supply and sanitation project. In Zambia the Bank promotes the Urban Restructuring and Water Project (including Lusaka Water and Sewerage Company) and the Mine Township Services Project.

10   G. Yirga-Hall (2001), 'Experiences and Challenges of Financing Water Systems in Africa', in *Volume II, Papers and Presentations, Reform of the Water Supply and Sanitation Sector in Africa Conference*, www.wsp.org, African Development Bank.

11   *The Economist*, 8 February 1992; the memo is available at http://www.whirledbank.org.

12   See, for example, J. Stiglitz (1998), 'More Instruments and Broader Goals: Moving Toward the Post-Washington Consensus', WIDER Annual Lecture, Helsinki, Finland, 7 January; and (2002), *Globalization and its Discontents*, London, Allen Lane. It is widely understood that Summers – as US Treasury Secretary – compelled James Wolfensohn to fire Stiglitz (who was then World Bank chief economist) in September 1999 once his objections to the Washington Consensus became sufficiently damaging.

13   The Kampala Statement was drafted at the World Bank and issued in mid-March 2001. It attempted to speak for 'a total of 270 participants drawn from government, the utilities (including the private sector), financial institutions, external support agencies, and civil society'. Quotations are from the final email version sent from the Bank on 14 March 2001.

14   These have often been cited in the 30 per cent range, payable in hard currency (i.e. if the local currency falls, then the profit rate is even higher). According to the African Development Bank (ADB), the South Africa Infrastructure Fund projection for before-tax Internal Rate of Returns of 26-7 per cent 'during SAIF's 15-year life in constant US dollar terms' assumes that '10 per cent of all investments will fail; 50 per cent of all investments will generate an IRR of 30 per cent; and 40 per cent of all investments will generate an IRR of 35 per cent'. To earn such high rates of return on infrastructure investments that are often long term in nature (often 40 years before full social and economic returns on investment are realized), and on top of that to compress the high earnings into the early stages of investment (on average 7.5 years, given that the SAIF will shut down after 15 years), and to do so using a wide range of social infrastructure investments, implies an extremely high cost-recovery burden for direct infrastructure recipients, or dramatic cost reductions at the level of the enterprise. See African Development Bank (1997), 'Investment Proposal: South Africa Infrastructure Investment Fund', ADB Private Sector Unit, Abidjan, p. 13, Annex 6. As noted below, the International Finance Corporation authorized a major investment in the SAIF, so these high profit rates are apparently consistent with the World Bank water-commodification strategy.

15   The statement argues, on the contrary, that multilateral and bilateral agencies 'are keen to support' privatization, and that 'In view of the limited budgetary resources in most African countries, external financing should be available to cover the operational deficit resulting from the lag between improved service and increased revenue during the initial years of PPP'. No mention is made of the lack of hard-currency revenue that comes from selling water services to low-income people, despite the need to repay the multilateral and bilateral financiers in hard currency.

16   The statement's only concession along these lines is 'Where price increases to cover costs and improve service are planned, these should be gradual and should follow service improvements to maintain public support'.

18   It is well known that there are public and merit good effects from provision of water and sanitation to the homes of low-income people. Instead of making a strong case for lifeline water provision, tellingly, the Kampala Statement offers only extremely shallow rhetoric on this point: 'While the role of the private sector should increase in most cases, the public aspects of water and sanitation services should not be compromised. The creation of an independent regulator and corresponding legislation before any major transfer of operational activity to the private sector can help to ensure the priority of the public interest through increased fairness, transparency, accountability and better monitoring of contract performance'.

19   World Bank (2000), *Sourcebook on Community Driven Development in the Africa Region: Community Action Programs*, Africa Region, Washington, DC, 17 March (signatories: Calisto Madavo, Jean-Louis Sarbib), Annex 2.

20   World Bank, *Sourcebook on Community Driven Development in the Africa Region*, Annex 2.

21   J. Pauw (2003), 'Metered to Death: How a Water Experiment Caused Riots and a Cholera Epidemic', Washington, DC, International Center for Investigative Journalism, Center for Public Integrity, 5 February.

22   World Bank (1999), *Country Assistance Strategy: South Africa*, Washington, DC, Annex C, p. 5.

23   J. Roome (1995), 'Water Pricing and Management: World Bank Presentation to the SA Water Conservation Conference', unpublished paper, South Africa, 2 October.

24   Alexandra residents (1998), 'Inspection Panel Claim regarding World Bank Involvement in the Lesotho Highlands Water Project'. Paper presented anonymously to the World Bank Inspection Panel, March, pa.1.10.

25   Roome, 'Water Pricing and Management: World Bank Presentation to the SA Water Conservation Conference', pp. 50-1.

26   Ketso Gordhan, the main city manager promoting neoliberal utilities pricing and privatization, turned down a World Bank job offer in late 2000. Instead, he became deputy chief executive of FirstRand, which included one of South Africa's most aggressively pro-privatization merchant banks.

27   Palmer Development Group (2001), 'Rand Water: Tariff Database Survey 2', Johannesburg, March, p. 8.

28   Adapted from Palmer Development Group, 'Rand Water: Tariff Database Survey 2', Table 14.

29 Information in this and the following paragraphs is from K. Mare (2001), 'Free Basic Water: Actual Tariff Structures in Rand Water Area of Supply', presentation to the Water Services Forum, Johannesburg, 18 July.

30 S. Masia, J. Walker, N. Mkaza, I. Harmond, M. Walters, K. Gray and J. Doyen (1998), 'External BoTT Review', joint report by the Department of Water Affairs and Forestry, World Bank, British Department for International Development and Unicef, Pretoria, November.

31 M. Drakeford (1998), 'Water Regulation and Pre-payment Meters', *Journal of Law and Society*, 25, 4.

32 Dwaf (1998), 'Compulsory National Standards Relating to the Provision of Water Services in Terms of Section 9(1)(a)', Memo CWS02161, Pretoria, 30 December, p. 2.

33 For example, an interview on the SABC TV show *Newsmakers*, 14 January 2001.

34 *Business Day*, 9 April 2001.

35 World Bank (2000), *Sourcebook on Community Driven Development in the Africa Region: Community Action Programs*, Annex 2.

36 Details provided in P. Bond (1998), 'Mozambican Parliament Questions Debt Management', *Sunday Independent*, 21 December; and see rebuttal letters from the Bank's Mozambique officer Phyllis Pomerantz on 24 January 1999, and from myself and Joe Hanlon on 7 February 1999, and 11 July 1999. See also C. Denny and L. Elliott (1999), 'Fund Admits Debt Plans Will Fail Poor', *Guardian*, 19 April.

37 International Monetary Fund (1999), *Mozambique: Enhanced Structural Adjustment Facility Framework Paper for April 1999-March 2002*, Washington, DC.

38 http://www.citizen.org/cmep/water .

8

Commodification of Public Goods: Water, the Source of Life

Hellen Grace Akwii Wangusa

Privatization usually refers to the full sale of state-owned assets, but it also includes various kinds of divestment of public duties to the private sector. This form of contracting out, introducing commercial principles and reducing government's role in providing some goods and services is what is generally understood as privatization.

Under Structural Adjustment Programmes (SAPs) privatization had always been one of the preconditions for loan access from the international financial institutions (IFIs) and it continues to be so under the Poverty Reduction Strategy Papers (PRSP) Policy Matrix. Under the PRSP, privatization includes services like water and electricity.

Besides reducing government expenditure, privatization is seen as a valid and effective means of rescuing non-performing public assets, ensuring efficiency and access, and containing corruption.

There are at least three models of water privatization:

1 Complete sale by governments of public water delivery and treatment systems to private corporations.
2 Long-term leases or concessions allowing corporations to take over the delivery of water services and collection revenues.
3 Corporations contracted by governments to manage water services for an administration fee.

Water Wars

Water is undeniably one of the most important natural resource today, especially as the world's water becomes more polluted and out of reach of the poor. The former vice-president of the World Bank, Ishmael Serageldi, predicted that the wars of the twenty-first century would be fought over water. True to this prediction, the first water war was fought in Bolivia in 2000 after the World Bank refused to renew a $25 million loan unless water services were privatized. The people of Cochabamba ran amok when water rates were hiked by a US-based corporation. Similar incidents took place in Lima, Peru, where the rich get away with 30 US cents for clean water while the water vendors pay an incredible $3 per cubic foot for unsafe water. Ironically, in spite of such foresight, and perhaps because of his position as chair of the Global Water Partnership, Mr Serageldi remains one of the prime movers for the privatization of water in developing countries.

In May 2000 *Fortune Magazine* stated: 'Water promises to be to the twenty-first century what oil was to the twentieth century: the precious commodity that determines the wealth of nations'. Its relative availability or scarcity already has an impact on virtually every aspect of life and form of development. Water is an unsubstitutable resource. Local communities have protected it and treated it as a public good that is sacred and beyond commercial value. According to an African proverb, water is the only thing one cannot deny even an enemy. The provision of water needs to be seen as basic and central to human and other forms of life. It should not be treated as a tradable asset.

The Water Debate
In rural areas of Africa debates about water focus on to whom water is seen to belong, to whom it is being allocated and whose rights are violated when it is considered for privatization. As with land, traditional practice values water because of the life it provides and contains. Water continues to be regarded as a resource that needs to be regulated rather than abused or commodified. In numerous traditions waters were known to have a spirit or spirits that set the rules or practices for water use and the extraction of its resources, such as fish. Those rules effectively acted as tariffs and quotas to regulate the use of water.

Governments and funding partners are focusing on increasing private sector participation in rural water provision as one of the ways of ensuring wider coverage. A number of water projects were awarded to private contractors in Uganda, for example. This was done in close collaboration with local District tender boards, which had proved themselves incapable of providing the very water services they are meant to oversee.

Private sector involvement in water also entails great emphasis on the construction of physical infrastructure (hardware), but not the mobilization of the community (software) to ensure sustainability. Whereas private sector involvement in water management may ensure coverage, availability, quality of water and efficiency of service, it certainly eliminates those who cannot afford the water. It eliminates women, who need to continue as the principle managers of water provision and decision making. Replacing women with mechanisms put in place by profit makers will not sustain the spiritual and environmental life of water sources, nor ensure continued access and efficient management of water sources and infrastructure.

Who Benefits from the Privatization of Water?
In Tanzania the Dar es Salaam Water and Sewerage Authority (DAWASA) was asked to privatize water. An article by Wole Akande describes how the Tanzanian government had to raise $145 million to upgrade DAWASA before it could be privatized. This effectively increased Tanzania's debt and reduced the chances of the poor to gain access to water and sanitation services. Some $47 million of that money was raised from the Africa Development Bank and the rest from the World Bank, the European Investment Bank and Agence Française de Développement. The project was meant to bring about improved

accessibility, quality, reliability and affordability of water and increase the well-being of the people by subsequently contributing to poverty reduction.

In Ghana five multinational corporations bid for the Tema Water Service. These corporations are known to have annual sales incomes that are higher than the GDP of Ghana. Some of them have questionable social and environmental records. This directly raises concerns about the capacity of the Ghanaian government to monitor, regulate or even hold these companies accountable should they go beyond national prescriptions on social or environmental issues.

> The anticipated increase in efficiency of utility companies, when it did occur, in most cases did not result from improved operations. Rather, the ratio of revenue to expenses rose as a result of price increases facilitated by virtual monopoly situations and weak government regulatory mechanisms.

Water: The Best Investment Sector

The market for water and sanitation is increasing globally. It is estimated to be an annual billion dollar industry 40 per cent of the size of the oil sector and one third larger than pharmaceuticals. The big water corporations take advantage of the power and tools of trade and investment in developing countries. They are the beneficiaries of the World Bank and IMF loans and grants.

> When the Suez, for example, took over the water operations in Buenos Aires, all but $30 million of the 1 billion required for investment in new infrastructure came from the World Bank, with assistance from the Inter American Development Bank and local Argentine banks.

The Polaris Institute (2003) asserts that in March 2001 the World Bank was the major overseas investor ($225 million) in a large water services privatization project in Thailand developed by Thames Water International.

Privatization of Water: A Condition for the Renewal of Loans

A random review reported by the Polaris Institute notes that IMF loans in 40 countries in 2000 revealed that 12 had loan conditions that imposed privatization of water or full cost recovery. This was the case in Tanzania. Nyamugasira and Rowden (2002) observe that while ownership of water supply and sanitation assets in Uganda will remain in the hands of government, under the World Bank's Poverty Reduction Strategy Credit (PRSC-1) Policy Matrix annex, plans are outlined to privatize the operations of the national water supply and sanitation services in the urban centres and have the service provided by management contracts with local and international private operators.

During the Poverty Eradication Action Plan (PEAP) that gave birth to the Uganda PRSP, civil society clearly did not call for the privatization of the water utility to international investors. Nevertheless the process of privatizing water is underway, with plans for end-use customers to pay for improvements before the utility is sold to foreign investors. The privatization of water in Uganda, in other words, can only take place once consumers have shouldered the burden of ensuring that the system is financed so that it is profitable even before it is sold. These changes also ensure that the cross-subsidies that had been built into the price tariff structure are unbundled. This means that there will be no provision in the privatized water system for wealthier consumers to subsidize services to the poor.

The involvement of the IFIs in financing private water corporations and using privatization as a condition for accessing loans is not only seen as unjust but also as an imposition that interferes with national decision making and in some instances disregards civil society's concerns and priorities. In addition, it is a process that pressurizes governments to be more accountable to the IFIs, not their citizens.

If gender analysis and civil society participation are disregarded over water management, governments will not be able to withstand the global industry and the enormous corporations that specialize in the privatization of water

REFERENCES

Nyamugasira, Warren and Rowden, Rick, 'New Strategies, Old Conditions: Do the New IMF and World Bank Loans Support Country's Poverty-Reduction Goals?', Kampala and Washington, DC, April 2002.
Polaris Institute, 'Global Water Grab: How Corporations are Planning to Take Control of Local Water Services', January 2003.

9

The World Bank's Water Policies

John Garrison

The World Bank has invested much funding and technical assistance in water over most of its history. The Bank also acknowledges the concerns expressed by the WCC regarding the Bank's water policies, and welcomes a frank and open debate about the issues. Like any large development agency, the Bank has and will make mistakes in the course of funding hundreds of new development projects every year, and will continue to learn lessons.

I grew up as the son of a Methodist missionary family in Brazil and always heard much about the WCC. I have also worked for both Protestant and Catholic church agencies, carrying out human rights and development work, and thus appreciate the leadership role of the WCC in such areas as ecumenism and social justice.

I presently work as a civil society specialist at the World Bank in Washington. I have been with the Bank for seven years, having spent five years in the Bank's office in Brasilia, Brazil, also working to improve Bank-civil society relations. While in Brazil, I maintained frequent contacts with Protestant and Catholic church agencies in order to promote a dialogue between them and the Bank around such common issues as macro-economic policies, agrarian reform and Aids.

I am not a water expert and neither am I familiar with the South African or Ugandan cases highlighted in previous essays. This essay will therefore be more general regarding the Bank's water strategy, policies and experience.

The World Bank's Civil Society Engagement Work

The World Bank first began to interact with civil society in the 1970s through dialogue with non-governmental organizations on environmental concerns. Today, the World Bank consults and collaborates with thousands of civil society organizations (CSOs) throughout the world, such as community-based organizations, indigenous people's organizations, NGOs, labour unions, faith-based groups, and foundations.

The experience of the World Bank has shown that the participation of CSOs in government development projects and programmes can enhance operational performance by contributing local knowledge, providing technical expertise and leveraging social capital. Further, CSOs can bring innovative ideas and solutions, as well as participatory approaches, to solving local problems. It is for this reason that the World Bank is increasingly supporting civil society through greater information sharing, skills training and grant funding.

The World Bank's Traditional Commitment to Water

Water is a key ingredient in development, with strong linkages to health, nutrition and the environment; moreover, life itself cannot exist without it. For this reason, it is important to acknowledge that important gains have been achieved over the last decades in providing populations throughout the world with greater access to water. It is estimated that over the past 20 years, 2.4 billion people have gained access to water and 600 million to sanitation, most of these low-income populations in both urban and rural settings. An estimated $60 billion dollars is invested in water access and distribution in developing countries each year. About 90 percent of this investment comes from domestic sources.

On the other hand, it is also estimated that over 1 billion people are still without potable water, and 2 billion people without sanitation, the great majority of these being the very poor in developing countries. Water resources are unequally distributed, poorly managed and quickly becoming a rare and disputed resource in many countries. For this reason, the decisions surrounding water – who has access and at what costs – can represent a complex political issue involving divergent interests and difficult policy choices. By 2025 it is estimated that 48 countries will experience water stress or scarcity (up from 29 today) affecting 1.4 billion people. One of the eight Millennium Development Goals – global development goals established by the United Nations and other development agencies in 2000 – is to halve by 2015 the proportion of people without sustainable access to safe drinking water. Another goal is to achieve significant improvement in the lives of 100 million slum-dwellers through improved sanitation by 2020.

Since its establishment in 1947, the World Bank has supported investments related to water access and distribution. The Bank understands that water is a key environmental, human and social resource without which development cannot occur. From 1993 to 2001 water represented 17 per cent of all Bank lending. The World Bank accounts for about 50 per cent of all external financing for water – about $3 billion a year. Currently, the Bank is supporting hundreds of water and sanitation projects (either through loans or technical assistance) in 106 countries totalling $17 billion dollars. It is also quite important to note that the great majority of these activities are geared to supporting the water and sanitation activities of the public sector, either through national or local governments.

As in other areas, such as agriculture, health and education, the principal partner of the World Bank has traditionally been governments. In addition to governments, the Bank has also supported (but on a much smaller scale) the water access and distribution efforts of private companies and community groups. Today, only 5 per cent of the Bank's private investments are in the water sector.

World Bank Water Policy

The Bank first developed a comprehensive water sector policy in 1993 when it published the Water Resources Management Policy Paper. This paper identified three major principles which have guided the Bank's water- and sanitation-related activities. First, the *ecological* principle framed water in the context of land management and environmental conservation. Among other aspects, it promoted the holistic idea that natural resource development activities should be carried out within a 'river basin' approach. The second principle was *institutional* and defended the idea that all stakeholders – governments, private sector, civil society and donor agencies – should participate in the design and implementation of water and nutrition initiatives. Third, the paper highlighted an *instrumental* principle which argued that water is an increasingly scarce resource that requires improved management and technology to ensure widespread access, particularly for the poor.

The Bank's semi-independent Operations Evaluation Department (OED) carried out and published in 2001 a review of the 1993 water paper. While OED recognized the value of the Bank's water strategy, it called for the Bank's water policies to be better grounded in local country contexts. That same year, the Bank's water and sanitation team began to draft an updated water strategy which would take into account not only the findings of the OED evaluation, but also the lessons learned from financing hundreds of water and sanitation projects over the past decade. As part of the process of drafting the strategy, Bank staff held consultation meetings with CSOs (NGOs, labour unions, community groups, academics) in six countries throughout the world: Nigeria, Yemen, Brazil, Philippines, India and the United States, as well as a web-based consultations process. The Bank's current Water Resources Sector Strategy was endorsed by the Bank's Board of Directors in February 2003. The current water strategy as well as the past policy papers and OED evaluation can be found on the Bank's website under 'water strategy'.

World Bank's Position and Experience on Water Privatization

We recognize that there is growing controversy around the issue of water privatization, and the Bank has tried to be quite open about dialoguing with CSOs about their concerns in this area. We not only acknowledge the concerns expressed by some in civil society that privatization results in less water access to the poor through higher rates, but also position ourselves clearly on the need to provide universal water coverage, particularly to the poor. With this in mind, there are three basic points to stress.

Improving the Capacity of the Public Sector to Deliver Clean Water

The Bank continues primarily to fund public provision of water through infrastructure loans, promoting improved management capacity and ongoing technical assistance. The great majority of Bank loans in this area are geared to the public sector and include investments in infrastructure, improved technology and strengthening the institutional capacity of government water utilities. It is important to stress that when the Bank does support private sector water initiatives, this also includes community water systems managed by local civil society organizations.

On the other hand, government ownership and management of water systems is no guarantee of quality, efficiency and universal coverage. There are many examples of public water companies around the world which are operated inefficiently, charge high rates and allow for significant rates of water loss through seepage and broken pipes. Further, it is not uncommon to find that public water companies in the developing world do not provide coverage to low-income neighbourhoods, yet, at the same time, favour high-income neighbourhoods through regressive subsidy policies.

The situation for rural communities is often even more precarious as basic water services (drinking water, catchments, irrigation, sanitation) are simply not available. As a matter of fact, due to these problems of access, the Bank has found that in some areas where water is managed by the public sector, water is *de facto* privatized, as low-income residents must pay private suppliers to obtain water, often paying ten times more than high-income residents who have water piped into their homes. This is the case in drought-prone areas such as northeast Brazil, which I know quite well, having lived there, where water is not only scarce but also politicians have been known to use access to water as political currency during elections.

Public-Private Partnerships
The Bank does not have an *a priori* or ideological position on privatization. It does not force governments to privatize their water utilities – through conditionalities – in order to favour business interests, as some Bank critics have alleged. As a matter of fact, the Bank has steadily reduced the use of conditionalities in its loans in general and in the water sector in particular. When the public sector is a sound provider, why privatize? Yet the Bank and governments do attempt to attract private sector investment when water service and access can benefit from this participation. The private sector can bring needed capital, greater management expertise and improved technologies to water utilities which may be experiencing operating deficits and structural inefficiencies. When the private sector is brought in, though, there must be adequate governmental regulatory control and provisions for appropriate rate scales, universal coverage and environmental protection.

In these instances what the Bank seeks is public-private partnerships for water delivery, as the public sector invariably maintains overall control and ownership of water as a natural resource. Within this context, private water delivery systems have worked well in many instances by improving the quality of water, increasing coverage and operating more efficiently. On the other hand, private companies can also fail – much like state-owned enterprises – through inefficiency and corruption, and this can occur where there is insufficient regulatory control by governments.

It is important to note that the participation of the non-governmental sector also includes civil society initiatives. Over the years the Bank has supported hundreds of community-operated water management systems – distribution, storage and irrigation – through its social funds and government-funded programmes. In addition to being a service provider, civil society should also play a consumer watchdog role to ensure that either the governmental or private service provider is providing adequate services.

Need to Guarantee Water Quality

More important than which sector provides water services – government, private sector, civil society – is the need to guarantee the quality, coverage and efficiency of the service. Further, it is key to ensure that clean water is made available to low-income communities in urban and rural areas. Whether water services should be free and/or subsidized to the poorest segments of the population through cross-subsidies or taxes should also be discussed, as the Bank also does not have a fixed position on this. Each country context needs to be taken into consideration and flexible public or public-private partnerships need to be developed based on the comparative advantages posed by each of the different sectors: government, private, civil society. Whatever water provider approach is adopted the one constant is the need for the government to regulate the water sector in order to ensure quality, coverage and sustainability.

WDR 2004 on Service Provision

A good example of how the World Bank views the provision of water services is the current research and consultations on the 2004 World Development Report (WDR) entitled 'Making Services Work for the Poor'. Each year the Bank produces a thematic report (the WDR) on a pressing development topic, such as poverty, sustainable development and governance. The report for 2004 analyses different experiences worldwide on how services are being provided by governments, the private sector and civil society in the areas of education, health and water, with a special focus on how these services can be better geared to serve the poor. As in the water area, the WDR report has found that the public sector continues to be the traditional provider of social services throughout the world, and that the major task therefore is to strengthen the government's ability to provide greater access to services to the poor.

The WDR report has also found that, more important than who provides services – government, the private sector or civil society – it is imperative to guarantee the quality, efficiency, coverage, sustainability, transparency and accountability of these services. Church or other civil society organizations, for instance, have traditionally provided a large percentage of educational and health services in many developing countries in Africa and Latin America. No one should be advocating reducing this important role played by civil society in social service provision. Likewise, the report has found that if the private sector, within a framework of strong government regulation, can provide quality water or health services, then governments should consider exploring public-private partnerships.

Conclusion
The Bank is strongly committed to water provision in its programmes around the world and is not dogmatic or ideological about how best water can be provided. While the Bank will continue primarily to fund public sector provision of water, a variety of public-private partnership approaches are being adopted when the country context warrants it. The most important consideration for the Bank is that the water service provider ensure water which is potable, sustainable and accessible to the poor. Finally, it is important to reiterate that the Bank welcomes this debate with civil society on how best to increase water access to the poor and looks forward to its continuation.

10

The International Concept of Wealth Creation and Social Justice

Ann Duncan

Growth, Poverty and Inequality

For the purpose of this essay, I will interpret the concepts of wealth creation and social justice as economic growth, with reducing poverty and inequality in developing countries.

The World Bank is no longer of the view that economic growth alone is sufficient for poverty reduction; instead, we take the view that economic growth is necessary, but not sufficient, for poverty reduction. We also acknowledge, as does the IMF, the links between inequality, poverty and growth. In its original paper on the Poverty Reduction and Growth Facility (the IMF's concessional lending instrument for low-income countries in support of Poverty Reduction Strategy (Papers)), the IMF stated: 'The new approach recognizes the increasing evidence that entrenched poverty and severe inequality in economic opportunities and asset endowments can themselves be impediments to growth.'

Absolute income poverty, defined as living on less than $1 per day, declined from 28 per cent in 1987 to 23 per cent in 1998. Significant progress was made in East Asia before the crisis, and was reversed only partially. But the numbers of poor have remained roughly constant, because of population growth. One billion two hundred million people continue to live on less than $1 per day, and 2.8 billion on less than $2 per day.

In East Asia it seems that growth has had a stronger impact on reducing poverty, compared with many other parts of the world, in large part – in my own view – because the growth took place in an environment where the degree of inequality in assets (especially in land and primary education) was significantly less than in other regions. Because a substantial number of the less well-off people were able to own land and get an education, they were able to enjoy the benefits of growth, especially in agricultural productivity and labour markets.

World Bank View Of 'Good' (Pro-Poor) Development Policy

It is often difficult to encapsulate the Bank's view of complex issues such as these, in that this view changes over time as the global community, ourselves included, learn more about what makes development work. I have chosen as the current articulation of World Bank views on these issues some extracts from a recent publication by our chief economist, Nicholas Stern. In his view, there are three important aspects to 'sensible development policy' and the role of international financial institutions in supporting this:

> We now understand better what good development policy is. A country's development strategy needs to include both policies to improve the investment climate, in order to raise productivity and speed employment and wage growth, and polices to equip and empower poor people to participate in growth.
>
> We understand that leadership and broad commitment to policies are central to the process of development. It is not enough to design good policies. If they are to be implemented successfully, those policies must have the support of both political leaders and substantial elements of the populace.
>
> We know more about how international financial institutions such as the World Bank can operate as agents of change. Development strategies need to be comprehensive. Lending should make careful, well-focused and sparing use of conditionality, which is rarely able to substitute for domestic ownership of a reform. No one agency can do everything – 'seeing the whole is not trying to do the whole'. Partnership between actors and agencies, based on comparative advantage, is crucial.
>
> Developing countries and donors alike have begun to internalize these lessons, and we are seeing the results of their efforts … Governments are concentrating more on what they must do well to spur development. Improvements in macro-economic stability and openness are being buttressed by improvements in other elements of the investment climate, including governance. And expansion of educational opportunity, along with the wave of democracy that has swept across the world in the past quarter-century, has led to at least some empowerment of poor people. For countries that have taken these steps, the result has been more rapid growth and progress in poverty reduction.
>
> We now share an understanding that state and market are not substitutes but complements: the state must lay the foundations for the market, if the market is to flourish and work its magic. Strong markets and the involvement of poor people in development require a well-functioning state.

Out of this recent thinking has emerged the new PRSP approach. Now, more and more Bank lending, policy advice and analytical work in low-income countries is in support of pro-poor development strategies, articulated through Poverty Reduction Strategy Papers. PRSPs are developed and owned by the country, usually led by government, in consultation with civil society and other key stakeholders. Bank lending/support for PRSPs is in the form of HIPC debt relief, investment lending (projects), and/or budget support (e.g. Poverty Reduction Support Credits, or other types of budget support). Our Country Assistance Strategy (CAS) is increasingly aligned behind and in support of the country's PRSP. For a recent review of progress in implementing the PRSP approach, see two papers produced jointly by the Bank and Fund staff (both available on our website):

1   'Review of the PRSP Approach', 27 March 2002
2   'PRSPs – Progress in Implementation', 11 September 2002

One of the most successful ways to empower and equip poor people is through investing in their own human capital – in their education and health. From fiscal year 1986 to fiscal year 2000 our annual lending to the social sectors (education, health, nutrition, population and social protection) increased by a factor of five, to $4,868 million.

The projects we support in these and several other sectors (e.g. rural water supply) are increasingly designed to empower the poor as clients/consumers of these services. Some notable examples of this approach have been the EDUCO community-managed schools project in El Salvador; the Balochistan Pilot Fellowships, that stimulate demand for rural girls' education in that province in Pakistan; and the Bangladesh Girls' Secondary Education project. Bank-supported projects in almost all sectors and countries are increasingly based on participation by users/clients/beneficiaries, which we believe is an important factor in the success of projects.

Empowering the poor is important not just in a project context, but also more widely through improvements in governance. An interesting example of more transparent governance has been started in Cameroon: under the HIPC programme, an independent monitoring system, which includes civil society as members, has been set up for monitoring the use of the debt relief savings. The recent wave of democracy and the massive growth in electronic communications over the last two decades or so has forced governments to become more transparent and accountable to their citizens. Over time, this trend should result in the poor gaining increasing control over and access to domestic markets and institutions.

Empowering developing countries – especially the low-income countries – in the international arena is also critical to improve social justice and improve living standards for the poor. The World Bank is making major efforts on the international stage to improve access to developed country markets for poor countries, and to reduce developed country subsidies to their own agricultural sectors: these subsidies result in lower prices for agricultural commodities, ultimately affecting the incomes of poor farmers in developing countries. The combined losses to developing countries of agricultural subsidies and restricted market access in the developed countries (especially for agriculture and textiles) is estimated to cost developing countries in the region of $300 billion per annum, or about six times the volume of official development assistance (about $50 billion per annum).

Conclusion

Over the last few decades the Bank has made significant changes in its understanding of the relationship between economic growth and poverty. This is now reflected in its advice to developing countries, its lending priorities and policies. There is a growing recognition that for sustainable poverty reduction, the poor need progressively more control over their own lives, and sustained opportunities to build their assets; this needs to take place in the context of fairer, more transparent and democratically accountable domestic and international governance; and in the context of institutions and markets that support, rather than undermine, their efforts.

These changes in thinking, the questioning, and the advance of our understanding together provide an opportunity and a challenge to the international development community. We now have an opportunity to 'raise our game' in the fight against poverty and, working together, with greater resources and better policies, to make real progress in reducing poverty. There are grounds for optimism – if an ever-greater need to work constructively in partnership with other actors in development, and to be continuously open to learning from each other.

11

Summary of Main Agreements and Decisions

Athena Peralta

Commonalities and Differences
The first seminar between the World Council of Churches, the International Monetary Fund and the World Bank helped to identify areas of commonality as well as issues of difference among the three institutions with respect to their mandates, development perspectives, concepts of social justice and views on privatization.

Overall, the WCC, IMF and World Bank – three international institutions that were established after the Second World War and have shaped development philosophy and policy to varying degrees – share the common objective of poverty eradication in a world facing the immense challenges of economic globalization. However, the three institutions have dissimilar operational values and approaches to achieving this objective.

In the interests of transparency, a decision was made to publish the papers presented during the seminar which show the different developmental perspectives of the three institutions. It is hoped that this will encourage feedback not only among the seminar participants, but also from constituencies that have been and continue to be directly affected by the development policies of these three institutions.

It was further proposed that the group reports highlighting the commonalities and differences of the three institutions be further sharpened by a smaller planning group in a concise summary of the seminar proceedings. The seminar proceedings will also be published in a dossier.

Issues to be Taken Forward in a Second Seminar
As a next step, the participants from the WCC, IMF and World Bank generally agreed that the process of dialogue between the three institutions should be continued in the form of a second collaborative seminar, notwithstanding continuing differences between the three institutions.

As intended, the plenary/group discussions brought to the fore a number of pressing concerns – ranging from the issue of participation, to the HIV-Aids pandemic – that call for joint clarification and analysis from the standpoints of the WCC, IMF and World Bank in a second seminar. However, it was decided that the second seminar would focus on four specific issues:

1 *Participation of civil society in development.* The issue of people's participation in development policy making, implementation, monitoring and evaluation will be looked at in terms of roles and processes, with emphasis on the external debt problem and the Poverty Reduction Strategy Paper (PRSP) approach of the IMF and World Bank.

2   *Institutional governance and accountability.* The need will be discussed for more democratic and representative governance of international institutions and accountability for their development policies and actions.
3   *Respective roles of public and private sectors in development.* Here, the roles/responsibilities of and interplay between states and markets in development policy and poverty eradication efforts will be explored. The question of how to deal with governments lacking in legitimacy will also be tackled.
4   *Challenges of globalization.* The following questions will be addressed, among others: What are the dynamics of the globalization process? Who are the key actors? What are the impacts in terms of growth and equity?

Planning for the Second Seminar

Venue, dates, participants, style/format and communication procedures for the second seminar were also decided on.

Since the WCC had offered hospitality in hosting the first seminar in Geneva, it was agreed that the IMF and World Bank would have their turn in hosting the second seminar, which would take place in the autumn of 2003 in Washington, DC. The exact dates of the second seminar would be finalized by a smaller planning group.

The importance of continuity in terms of participation was stressed in order to build on gains already made during the first seminar. It was therefore suggested that the second seminar should generally be composed of the participants to the first seminar in Geneva. As with the first seminar, the institutions would pay for the travel and accommodation of their own participants.

Presentations and plenary and group discussions would continue to be utilized in the second seminar to help clarify and deepen analyses of issues for discussion. There was a recommendation to present specific country cases in dealing with the issues. Role-playing was also suggested as a possible activity for the second seminar.

Transparency and publicity – internally and externally – were again emphasized. To enable better preparation and a more informed and meaningful exchange between the WCC, IMF and World Bank, it was suggested that presentations and papers for the second seminar be shared among speakers and participants before the seminar dates, allowing ample time for reaction.

Finally, to keep the process of dialogue between the three institutions alive between seminars and meetings, a reminder was made to share information and reactions to development issues.

Appendix A

Meditation in the Chapel, Ecumenical Centre: A Change of Heart is Possible

Aruna Gnanadason

Genesis 50: 15-21

> Let us pray: God, whose insistent call disturbs our settled lives, give us discernment to hear your word, grace to relinquish our own thoughts and courage to follow wherever you lead. Amen.

The Bible is replete with stories that demonstrate that a change of heart is possible. The story of Joseph is one such story. Ten men, who do the most evil and hateful things to their own brother so as to destroy him, recognize at the end that injustice does not pay. They are made to recognize that community and just relationships are what matters.

Let me remind you of the story. Joseph, the beloved son of Jacob, is a dreamer as well as being an interpreter of dreams. The Bible tells us that he was his father's favourite. He had been given a coat by his father – a special coat of many colours, some versions of the Bible tell us. This special relationship between father and son makes the other brothers resent Joseph. But as if this is not enough, Joseph makes matters worse – he provokes his eleven brothers to anger by telling them of his dreams. In Joseph's first dream, he and his brothers are tying the sheaves in the field. His sheaf rises and their sheaves bow down to his sheaf. In his second dream, not only his eleven brothers but also his father and mother bow down to him – in this dream the sun and the moon and eleven stars bow down to him. The brothers are angry at this arrogance and they plot their vengeance – in fact they plan to kill Joseph. The use of power, of violence (and in our world today this translates as military power), as an option seems to be the way out for them. However, Rueben, one of the brothers, takes pity on Joseph and pleads with them not to kill him. So they throw him into a deep pit, with no water or food, and plan to tell their father that he is dead. But then they decide that it would be a good commercial proposition if they sold him as a slave to some Ishmaelite merchants who are passing by. They make on this sale 20 pieces of silver. Later, the Ishmaelite merchants sell Joseph into slavery in Egypt, to Potiphar, one of the Pharaoh's officials.

The story meanders through many details, which are not of relevance just now. What saves Joseph finally is the fact that he is the interpreter of dreams. He is called on to interpret the dreams of the Pharaoh himself. Joseph predicts seven good years with good harvests, followed by seven years of famine. By virtue of the good advice he gives the Pharaoh, he is elevated into a position of authority in the government – he is made governor of a region. Joseph is given the responsibility to ensure that the food grains are stored well and sold in a controlled manner, so that the country can be saved from the impending famine, just as he had predicted in interpreting the Pharaoh's dream.

The Bible tells us that there were indeed seven years of good agricultural production and then seven years of famine in the region, including in Canaan, where Jacob and his sons are living. Only Egypt is prepared for the famine years. Hearing that there is grain available in Egypt, Jacob sends ten of his sons there to buy grain. He keeps back with him his youngest son Benjamin. The ten men happen to come to the region where Joseph their brother is governor. Joseph recognizes his brothers immediately, but they do not recognize him and they bow down in front of him and beg for his help (just as he had dreamt).

Again, the story takes many turns until finally Joseph reveals himself to them as their brother. To their great surprise he tells them not to fret for what they had done to him. God had sent him ahead to create the possibility for all of them to live, he says. He embraces them and gives them all the food they need – he makes them understand there is no ill-feeling between brothers.

But it is they who are uncertain until the end. When their father dies they are worried that Joseph will now pay them back for the evil they had done by selling him and getting rid of him in their fit of jealousy. The brothers react in three different ways when they appeal to Joseph for mercy.

They appeal to Joseph by weeping – taking a victim approach. The brothers are here ready to accept whatever Joseph is willing to give them. Sometimes, those in power prefer that the vulnerable, the ones in need, should take this victim approach and silently accept what is good for them. Why aren't the poor grateful for the crumbs, the charity, that the rich give them out of the goodness of their hearts? Why are they seeking more? This is what we are often asked, when the poor of our world resist injustice. The churches are good at acts of charity. But then the question we need to ask ourselves in the next two days is whether charitable acts, as noble as they are, can ever transform deeply embedded structural injustices.

However, the brothers do not trust that this tack will work and they react in the second way: instilling in Joseph the power we would give to kings. They fall at his feet and ask him to accept them as his slaves. Here we have an 'empire' image: a position of power and control to which those with economic and political power easily succumb. We see this empire ideology being played out so strongly in our world today – where centres of economic, political and military power bring the weak to their knees. And again, those who resist the accumulation of power in the hands of a few empire builders are considered a problem – even by the churches!

Perhaps what touches Joseph the most is his brothers' appeal to him on the basis of their relationship: they are brothers, sons of the same father, and he must forgive them. It is a familial approach they take here in their longing for justice and community. We can recognize in each other our common humanity. On hearing this appeal, Joseph weeps, the Bible tells us. He urges his brothers not to be afraid and asks, 'Am I in the place of God?' Joseph sheds all semblance of power. He rejects any attempt to make him the centre of attention. Don't make a God of me, he says. These are indeed brave words for a man who could have abused his power – in our world today we see just how easily some do play God! Joseph, on the other hand, urges them to recognize God's hand in the protection of the little ones of the world. In fact, he is challenging them to a change of heart – no one is beyond the grace of God.

As we reflect together in the next few days, let us not forget this message from a God who cares for the 'little ones' in our world – the Josephs of our world; the ones who have for all their lives lived in a world of injustice; a world where the right to life and justice is a dream unfulfilled. Let us not forget in the next two days that the wisdom for a change could come from the most unlikely sources. And as we explore together the meaning of poverty, of wealth, of development, and as we reflect on the policies and plans we have made for decades now which do not seem to change the lives of millions in our world, in spite of all we do – let us not forget that a change of heart is possible. Let us not forget that even the most vulnerable ones in our world are not beyond the grace of a loving and compassionate God who, in tenderness, continuously reassures them not to be afraid. Amen.

Meditation in the Chapel, Ecumenical Centre: Water and the Economy

Mark 10: 17-22

Park Seong-Won

Here are four stories which might give us some kind of idea for our ongoing discussion.

The first story is the wisdom of Lao Tsze. As you may know, Lao Tsze is the founder of Taoism. In his book, he highly praises the value of water, particularly the metaphysical or philosophical value of water, beyond its physical value. As we all know, water never flows from the low level to the high. It always flows from the high level down to the low level. Water permeates every corner of available space, even the very hidden spaces at the lowest level. In such a way, water provides a substantial element for life. One of the most obvious illustrations of this phenomenon can be found in the relation between a tree and water.

However, the flow of water is not the same as the 'trickle-down' notion in the modern economy. When water flows down to the low level, the high level empties itself in order to fill the lower level. In fact, in this way, life at the top is also possible when there is life in the lower part; we can also observe this mechanism in the roots which are vital for the life of a tree.

This thought leads me to the second story, taken from a story about John Calvin. As you again may know, Calvin was one of the most prominent leaders of the Reformation movement in Geneva in the sixteenth century. Many people think that he and Calvinism made a substantial contribution to capitalism. However, this is not entirely true and is perhaps due to Max Weber's interpretation of Calvinism, not to Calvin himself. Calvin's concern was not focused on capitalism as such.

Among many economic principles, Calvin proposed an inclusive economy rather than an exclusive economy, a solidarity economy rather than a competitive economy, and an economy based on love and grace rather than an economy based on greed and profit making. The primary purpose of these principles was to make sure of the life of the poor in what we might call a poor-friendly economy.

What is directly related to the first story is that wealth should flow from the rich to the poor, not from the poor to the rich. The redistribution should go from the richer towards the poorer. In today's economic system we see the opposite movement of wealth. The richer become richer and richer, while the poor become poorer and poorer. Today, wealth flows from the poor to the rich.

This leads to the third story, taken from the text that we read this morning. The rich young man asked Jesus for a response on how to obtain eternal life. This is a profound metaphysical question, but Jesus' answer was quite concrete. After checking whether the rich young man had observed all the commandments, which he had done perfectly, Jesus gave him the following answer: 'You lack one thing; go and sell what you own, and give the money to the poor and you will have treasure in heaven; then come, follow me.'

The rich young man was shocked by this recommendation of Jesus and went away grieving. Interesting also is the additional comment that Jesus made further down in the text: 'It is easier for a camel to go through the eye of a needle than for someone who is rich to enter the kingdom of God' (Mark 10: 25). This means that caring for the poor is a precondition for the salvation of the rich.

In fact, Calvin calls the rich 'the ministers of the poor' and the poor the 'vicars of Christ', a dramatic way of saying that the poor are sent by God to the rich in order to test their faith and charity. This does not mean that the rich have a responsibility to be generous to the poor in a paternalistic way. What God wants to see here is strong solidarity between the rich and the poor so that both can enjoy the grace and love that God has given to our community.

The fourth story is the Asian understanding of the economy. The Chinese character for 'economy' is taken from the following sentence: *Kyung Sei Jae Min.*

Kyung means to manage; Sei means the world; Jae literally means to save, to make life possible and sustainable; Min means people. The literal meaning of the Chinese character for 'economy' is 'To save people by managing the world'. If I express this in a Western way, it would mean 'To make people's lives possible and sustainable by managing the world'. The focus here is to make the lives of people possible and sustainable. The economy and market should be managed or regulated so that it makes sure of the lives of people. If the lives of people are endangered, the economy is failing to achieve its mandate.

There is also an interesting idea related to the Chinese character for 'peace'. *Pyeong Hwa*, the Chinese character for peace, consists of two words, one of which means 'to level' or 'to equalize' and the other means 'grains to every mouth'. 'Peace' in Chinese characters is therefore 'To distribute equally grains to every mouth'. Economic equity is a sound condition for peace.

Today, we have lost the primary mandate of our vision on the economy. Today, we have forgotten such a simple and fundamental way to achieve security and peace. It is highly important to put people and life at the heart of our economic activities. Let us not forget about the wisdom of water in organizing today's global economy. Amen.

Appendix B

List of Participants in the First WCC, World Bank and IMF Seminar, February 2003

Brian Ames, International Monetary Fund
Shyamala Ariarajah, KAIROS Global Association for Investment Ethic
Karen Bloomquist, Lutheran World Federation
Patrick Bond
Pamela K. Brubaker, California Lutheran University
Ann Duncan, World Bank
John Garrison, World Bank
Aruna Gnanadason, World Council of Churches
Bob Goudzwaard
Graham Hacche, International Monetary Fund
Michiel Hardon, World Council of Churches
Linda Hartke, Ecumenical Advocacy Alliance
Arntraud Hartmann, World Bank
Peter S. Heller, International Monetary Fund
Beverly Keene, Dialogo 2000
Jane Kelsey, Law School, Auckland University
Alexei Kireyev, International Monetary Fund
Erik Lysén, Church of Sweden
Katherine Marshall, World Bank
Juan Michel, World Council of Churches
Rogate R. Mshana, World Council of Churches
Athena Peralta, World Council of Churches
Bassirou Sarr, International Monetary Fund
Park Seong-Won, World Council of Reformed Churches
Alfredo Sfeir-Younis, World Bank
Wendy Tyndale, World Faith Development Dialogue
Robert van Drimmelen, Aprodev
Sofia Walan, Christian Council of Sweden
Hellen Grace Akwii Wangusa, African Women's Economic Policy Network
Peter Weiderud, World Council of Churches
Margarita E. Witte-Rang, Oikos
Fabrizio Zarcone, World Bank

L'impression et le façonnage ont été réalisés
à l'Imprimerie LUSSAUD - 85200 Fontenay-le-Comte

Dépôt légal 2e trimestre 2004 - n° 3739 – N° d'impression : 203522